DESIGNING COMPLEX ORGANIZATIONS

JAY GALBRAITH

*The European Institute for
Advanced Studies in Management*

Addison-Wesley Publishing Company
Reading, Massachusetts
Menlo Park, California • London • Don Mills, Ontario

This book is in the Addison-Wesley series:

ORGANIZATION DEVELOPMENT

Editors
Edgar H. Schein
Richard Beckhard
Warren G. Bennis

Copyright © 1973 by Addison-Wesley Publishing Company, Inc.
Philippines copyright 1973 by Addison-Wesley Publishing Company, Inc.

Library of Congress Catalog Card No. 72-11887

ISBN 0-201-02559-0
ABCDEFGHIJ-CO-79876543

FOREWORD

Since the publication of the original series of six books on organization development (OD), this field has grown rapidly. No longer is it a field in search of a clear self-definition. We now find a large number of books and articles on OD and many competing models of what OD is and should be. All this proliferation of conceptualizing, empirical research, and description of new OD tools is a healthy and welcome development. Apparently, organizations have found that concepts and techniques of organization development are useful and viable, and schools have found that the theory and practice of planned change in organizations is a useful part of their curriculum.

One area of concern that received insufficient attention in the original series was the relationship of the organization to its *environment.* Only the Lawrence and Lorsch volume dealt explicitly with this problem, yet it continues to be one of the most fruitful areas for further exploration. The environment is changing rapidly, and the impact of this change on organizational structure and process must be clearly understood if OD efforts are to remain relevant to organizational realities. The present set of three books takes three quite different perspectives toward this problem in the hope of further stimulating thought and practice.

At the most general level, one can think of the environment as generating a set of values which influence organizational functioning and managerial thought. Roeber has written in a broad vein what some of these value changes have been in the last several decades and how such changes have influenced managerial thinking. At a somewhat more specific level, the environment is a source of information for an organization, and the organization must learn how to process increasingly larger quantities and more complex categories of information. Galbraith addresses this problem by relating how different forms of organization structure have evolved in response to increasingly difficult problems of information processing. Although the analysis of organization structure has always been a difficult problem to deal with systematically, Galbraith has found a way to bring order to this complex area by building on previous theories and integrating them around his information-processing view of organizations.

The environment can also be thought of in more concrete physical terms. Work takes place in a physical environment and is influenced by the nature of that physical environment. Yet virtually no attention is paid to the systematic analysis and manipulation of this portion of the environment. Steele gives us a clear view of some of the issues, provides a diagnostic scheme for the analysis of the environment, and suggests how organizations can set about to create physical environments which are more congruent with organizational goals.

As in our first series, we have not attempted to integrate the work of the different authors. Each gives us his view and his particular perspective on how to use that view to improve organizational functioning. We hope that the reader will be stimulated by these views to better understand his own organization and to begin some new organization development efforts.

March 1973   Edgar H. Schein
                                                            Richard Beckhard
                                                            Warren G. Bennis

PREFACE

This book is an attempt to present an analytical framework of the design of organizations and particularly of types of organizations which apply lateral decision processes or matrix forms. These forms are becoming quite pervasive in all types of organizations, and yet there is little systematic public knowledge about them. My intent is to help fill in this knowledge gap.

The implicit assumption underlying the use of matrix designs is that we cannot find authority structures in the form of product divisions, regional departments, programs, functions, etc., which will encompass all the activities which require coordination. There is a major defect in any choice we might make. In addition these defects may not be corrected by the informal organization which can arise to work across lines of authority. In organizations such as multinational organizations where there are physical separations, language differences, and cultural differences, the informal processes do not always arise spontaneously out of the needs of the task. I assume that if these lateral processes do not arise spontaneously they can be designed. The framework created in this book attempts to identify the types of matrix designs and the conditions under which they are appropriate. In addition to the presentation and justification of the framework, several cases illustrating applications are described and analyzed.

The book is primarily but not exclusively devoted to matrix designs. There are other design alternatives. These are juxtaposed with the matrix designs to give the larger context in which a design choice is made. These alternatives along with reward system designs are treated in my larger book, *Organization Design: An Information Processing View,* also published by Addison-Wesley.

The reader needs to be warned in several ways before reading the text. First, a casual reading would lead the reader to believe that we know more than we do about organizations. I prefer a style which is assertive rather than one which prefaces each statement by, "It is hypothesized that. . . . " I tend to fill in the holes in the data with my own interpretations. This is both a strength and a weakness of the framework. The reader should be forewarned in either case. But I can say that if I had to choose a design, the framework describes how I would choose.

The second feature of the text is that it is abstract. The practical man of affairs is asked to wait for the example cases and the latter part of the book. I have attempted to bring theory to bear on design issues, yet be general enough so that the framework can be applied to different types of organizations. However, since most of my experience and all my examples are from manufacturing organizations, the application to other organizations is still difficult. Thus while I believe that the framework can be applied to hospitals, for example, I have not shown how one applies it.

A third warning is that reader will find nothing new. Most of the designs and issues have been with us for some time. What I have tried to do is to synthesize a number of phenomena which are usually treated separately. I feel this synthesis can be based on some of the empirical studies that are available. The reader will like or dislike this book depending on how the synthesizing framework strikes him or her. It is this synthesis which is the contribution, if any, that this book makes.

I have drawn upon the ideas of many people in writing this book but I must mention two. I have been influenced by James D. Thompson. It was he who influenced me to begin studying organizations and provided a basis for some of the content. The other person is Herbert Simon. There are times when it seems to me that I have merely rewritten his thinking on the basis of the last ten years' empirical evidence. The footnotes do not give sufficient credit to either of these two men.

I must also thank my family for forgoing the necessary number of ski trips to allow me to finish the book. And finally to Michel Kilduff and Sandy Peeters, who distinguished my m's, n's, and u's.

Brussels, Belgium   J. R. G.
March 1973

CONTENTS

Chapter 1
INTRODUCTION

The field of organization development in general and to some degree this series in particular has developed out of an emphasis on change and on planned change. This book on organization design offers a different but complementary set of ideas. The differences and complementarities are best illustrated by a schematic, as shown in Figure 1.

Assume it is possible to represent the important features of an organization by a circle. Then at some moment our organization is

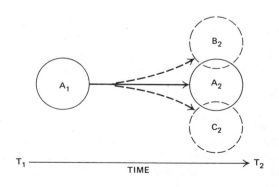

Figure 1

represented by A_1. If left alone the forces already set in motion will drive the organization to some state A_2. If the people or groups in positions of influence are dissatisfied with the current state of affairs they may want to intervene and divert the organization's path toward B_2 or toward C_2. Much of the organization development literature is concerned with planned interventions and strategies for diverting the organization. But what are these states B_2, C_2, or D_2 toward which the organization can be diverted? These states are different forms of organization. The purpose of this book is to present a model with which we can identify and evaluate these alternative organizational forms.

CONTINGENCY THEORY

The design of organization structures is an old topic which has passed through a number of stages of inquiry. The current stage, as usual, is characterized by a number of schools of thought. The author finds himself in a school labeled as contingency theory. This theory is based on two conclusions drawn primarily from large-scale empirical studies.

1. There is no one best way to organize.

2. Any way of organizing is not equally effective.

Thus we can observe a wide range of effective organizations but their differences are not random. The form of organization makes a difference. All of which suggests a new set of questions. On what factors does the choice of organization form depend? What are the characteristics of organizational contexts which appear to make a difference? Research in the past ten years suggests several.

One of the first studies was performed by Burns and Stalker.[1] In observing 20 British and Scottish firms they identified two types of organization—organic and mechanistic. More important, they suggested that each was effective. The mechanistic form was effective in stable markets, while the organic was effective in rapidly changing markets and technologies.

In another study of 100 British firms, Woodward found a relation between structure and effectiveness only when the production technology was controlled.[2] Among other features, small-batch, custom-design technologies used flat organizations with relative little staff personnel.

Mass-production, stable technologies were tall with a large indirect labor component.

Alfred Chandler, using the methodology of comparative historical analysis, studied over 70 of America's largest industrial firms.[3] He was interested in the creation and spread of the decentralized multidivisional structure. He discovered that the multidivisional form was not uniformly adopted throughout industry. The determining factor appeared to be the growth strategy of the firm. Those firms pursuing a growth strategy in a single industry utilized the centralized functional form, while those pursuing growth through diversification assumed the decentralized product division form or geographical division form. These results have been confirmed and extended to international diversification in a recent study of 170 American firms.[4]

A study by Richard Hall, a sociologist, has produced an interesting variation.[5] The previous studies accounted for variations in structure between organizations by analyzing task predictability and diversity. Hall pointed out that the same differences in task predictability occurred within as well as between organizations. Using categories conceptually equivalent to Burns and Stalker's mechanistic and organic types, Hall found the predicted internal structure variation. That is, the research and development departments had organic forms, while the production departments approximated the mechanistic form. Hall's study adds greatly to the generality of the previous findings.

The last study to be described here is one which combines the approaches of the previously mentioned studies.[6] Lawrence and Lorsch's proposition was that there are two considerations in the organization design problem. The first is to organize each subtask in a manner which facilitates the effective performance of that subtask. To the extent that subtasks vary in their predictability, different structures should be used. It also follows that different cognitive and emotional orientations will arise in the different structures. This aspect of the design problem is called *differentiation.*

The other aspect of the design problem is to provide for the *integration* of the differentiated subtasks so as to achieve successful completion of the whole task. The appropriate way to achieve integration depends first upon the degree of differentiation, since the greater the differences between two subtasks the more difficult it is to achieve effective collaboration. Also the integration problem varies with the rate at which new products are being introduced. This approach would account for task predictability differences which exist between and within organizations.

The results of the study, carried out with ten organizations in three industries, strongly support the propositions. That is, the successful organizations had differentiated internal structures when the subtasks varied in predictability. They also adopted integrating mechanisms in proportion to the amount of differentiation and the amount of new product introduction. The study confirms again the proposition that the predictability of the task is a basic conditioning variable in the choice of organizational forms.

Several other studies could be added to the list but the results would be the same.[7] All lead to the conclusion that the best way to organize is contingent upon the uncertainty and diversity of the basic task being performed by the organizational unit.[8] What remains to be done is to explain why uncertainty should have such an effect and to relate uncertainty to the design policy variables.

UNCERTAINTY AND INFORMATION

The basis of the design framework presented in this book is the proposition that the greater the uncertainty of the task, the greater the amount of information that has to be processed between decision makers during its execution. If the task is well understood prior to performing it, much of the activity can be preplanned. If it is not understood, then during the actual execution of the task more knowledge is acquired which leads to changes in resource allocations, schedules, and priorities. All these changes require information processing *during* task performance. Therefore *the greater the task uncertainty, the greater the amount of information that must be processed among decision makers during task execution in order to achieve a given level of performance.*

The basic effect of uncertainty is to limit the ability of the organization to preplan or to make decisions about activities in advance of their execution. Therefore it is hypothesized that the observed variations in organizational forms are actually variations in the strategies of organizations to (1) increase their ability to preplan, (2) increase their flexibility to adapt to their inability to preplan, or (3) to decrease the level of performance required for continued viability. Which strategy is chosen depends on the amount of uncertainty and the relative costs of the strategies. The function of the design framework is to identify these strategies and their costs.

Before articulating the design framework in the next chapter, we need to clarify the concepts of information and uncertainty.[9] *Uncertainty is defined as the difference between the amount of information required to perform the task and the amount of information already possessed by the organization.* Thus the amount of task uncertainty is a result of the combination of a specific task and a specific organization. The amount of information needed to perform a task is a function of (1) the *diversity of the outputs* provided as measured by the number of different products, services or clients, (2) the number of different *input resources* utilized as measured by the number of different technical specialties on a project, number of different machine centers in a factory, etc., and (3) the *level of goal difficulty* or performance as measured by some efficiency criterion such as percentage of machine utilization. The greater the diversity of outputs, number of resources, and level of performance, the greater the number of factors and interactions between factors that must be considered simultaneously when making decisions. The organization may not, however, possess the necessary amount of information. Uncertainty is the relative amount of information that must be acquired during task performance. It is relative to the amount of information required and the amount already possessed by the organization.

It is not uncertainty per se that is of interest. It is information processing, and specifically information processing during actual task execution, that is the key concept. It was suggested earlier that in predictable situations most of the coordination could be planned in advance of task execution. It is not implied that there is no information processing in this preplanning. There is usually a great deal, depending on the division of labor, diversity of outputs, and level of performance. For example, a great deal of information is necessary to balance the several thousand jobs along the automobile assembly line. Here the work is divided into thousands of highly interdependent subtasks. The line produces many diverse models and sizes, and it runs at a high level of efficiency. The result is that when decisions are made about rate of production or model mix, the impact of that decision on every job must be taken into account. This is a complicated decision known as the assembly line balancing problem. However, if customer demand, labor skills, and technology are predictable, there is little information to be processed after the line has been balanced.

In the case of uncertainty, the organization does not know the total demand, or the mix of station wagons, sedans, and convertibles. However, the organization estimates these factors, treats them as certainty equivalents, and processes them as in the certainty case in order to balance the line. But the estimates will probably be wrong. Customers will order more or fewer automobiles and proportionally more or fewer station wagons than initially estimated. When the organization changes its production rate it must rebalance all several thousand jobs along the line. It must process all that information again. The same issues arise as engineers create new process and product designs during the year. The line requires more rebalancing and more information processing. As the volume of information becomes substantial, the organization either finds ways to process the information or discovers ways to avoid having to do so. The framework presented in this book identifies explicitly how the organization can make these choices.

SUMMARY

This first chapter has very briefly presented a contingency theory basis for organization design decisions. The degree of task uncertainty was identified as the key variable on which the alternative designs are contingent. It was hypothesized that this is because alternative organization forms represent alternative capacities for processing information. The concepts of uncertainty and information were also briefly defined.

In the next chapter, a mechanistic model is introduced to illustrate how organizations can be conceived of as information-processing networks; this model provides a basis for the remainder of the book. Then the alternative strategies for dealing with information processing are related. Most of the book is devoted to so-called matrix designs. The theory and case illustrations make up the last half of the book.

NOTES

1. Tom Burns and G. M. Stalker, *The Management of Innovation* (London: Tavistock Publications, 1961).
2. Joan Woodward, *Industrial Organization: Theory and Practice* (London: Oxford University Press, 1965).
3. Alfred Chandler, *Strategy and Structure* (Garden City, N.Y.: Anchor Books, 1966).

4. Lawrence E. Fouraker and John M. Stopford, "Organizational Structure and the Multinational Strategy," *Administrative Science Quarterly,* June 1968, pp. 47–64.
5. Richard H. Hall, "Intraorganizational Structure Variation," *Administrative Science Quarterly,* December 1962, pp. 295–308.
6. Paul R. Lawrence and Jay W. Lorsch, *Organization and Environment* (Boston: Division of Research, Harvard Business School, 1967).
7. Jerald Hage and Michael Aiken, "Routine Technology, Social Structure and Organizational Goals," *Administrative Science Quarterly* **14** (1969), 366–377; and Robert B. Duncan, "Characteristics of Organizational Environments and Perceived Environmental Uncertainty," *Administrative Science Quarterly,* September 1972, pp. 313–327.
8. It should be kept in mind that there are other points of view on contingent variables. Some suggest size is the most important. See, for example, D. S. Pugh, D. J. Hickson, C. R. Hinings and C. Turner, "The Context of Organization Structure," *Administrative Science Quarterly* **14** (1969), 91–114.
9. For a more complete statement see Jay R. Galbraith, *Organization Design* (Reading, Mass.: Addison-Wesley), forthcoming.

Chapter 2
INFORMATION PROCESSING MODEL

In this chapter the basic model is created and the overall structure of the framework is outlined. Subsequent chapters will expand the major strategies put forth in the framework. Of necessity, the remainder of the chapter is fairly abstract. The purpose is to conceive of organizations as information-processing networks and to explain why and through what mechanisms uncertainty and information relate to structure. In order to accomplish this explanation, the basic bureaucratic mechanical model is created. The value of the model is not that it describes reality but that it creates a basis from which various strategies are formed to adapt the bureaucratic structure for handling greater complexity.

MECHANISTIC MODEL

In order to develop the model and the design strategies, assume that we have a task which requires several thousand employees divided among many subtasks. For example, the task of designing and manufacturing an aircraft or space capsule requires a group to design the capsule, a group to design the manufacturing methods, a group to fabricate parts and components, a group to assemble the parts, and a group to test the completed unit. The result is a division of labor which involves considerable interdependence and therefore coordination among the groups. The workflow is shown schematically in Figure 2.

In order to complete the task at a high level of performance, the activities that take place in the various groups must be coordinated. The behavior of the product design engineer must be consistent with the behavior of the process design engineers, etc. Although the behavior of several thousand people must be coordinated, it is impossible for all of them to communicate with each other. The organization is simply too large to permit face-to-face communication to be the mechanism for coordination. The organization design problem is to create mechanisms by which an integrated pattern of behavior can be obtained across all the interdependent groups. In order to see what these mechanisms are and the conditions under which they are appropriate, let us start with a very predictable task and slowly increase the degree of task uncertainty.

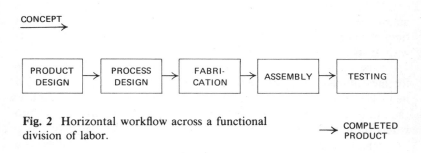

Fig. 2 Horizontal workflow across a functional division of labor.

First we have a task, like the one represented in Figure 2, in which there is a high degree of division of labor, a high level of performance, and relatively large size. A good deal of information must be processed to coordinate the interdependent subtasks. As the degree of uncertainty increases, the amount of information processing during task execution increases. Organizations must evolve strategies to process the greater amount of information necessary to maintain the level of performance. Let us follow the history of a fictitious organization performing the task represented in Figure 2 and observe the mechanisms that are created to deal with increasing information loads caused by increasing task uncertainty.

Rules, Programs, Procedures

The simplest method of coordinating interdependent subtasks is to specify the necessary behaviors in advance of their execution in the form of rules or programs.[1] In order to make effective use of programs, the organization's employees are taught the job-related situations with which they will be faced and the behaviors appropriate to those situations. Then as situations arise daily, the employees act out the behaviors appropriate to the situations. If everyone adopts the appropriate behavior the resultant aggregate response is an integrated or coordinated pattern of behavior.

The primary virtue of rules is that they eliminate the need for further communication among the subunits. If an organization has hundreds of employees, they cannot all communicate with each other in order to guarantee coordinated action. To the extent that the job-related situations can be anticipated in advance and rules derived for them, integrated activity is guaranteed without communication. These rules and programs perform the same functions for organizations that habits perform for individuals. They eliminate the need for treating each situation as new. The amount of communication and decision making is reduced each time a situation is repeatedly encountered. In addition, rules provide a stability to the organization's operations. As people come and go through an organization, the rules provide a memory for handling routine situations.

The best example of a programmed task is the automobile assembly operation. Each employee learns a specific set of behaviors for each possible situation he will face, e.g., station wagon, convertible, deluxe sedan, standard sedan, etc. For assembly operations the programs and procedures are created by engineers. In other situations individuals simply program themselves. That is, after confronting the same situation many times, individuals coordinate their behavior by following the same approach as in the past. Many standard operating procedures arise in this manner.

The use of rules and programs as coordination devices is limited, however. It is limited to those job-related situations which can be anticipated in advance and to which an appropriate response can be identified. As the organization faces new and different situations, the use of rules must be supplemented by other integrating devices.

Hierarchy

As the organization that depends on rules encounters situations it has not faced before, it has no ready-made response. When a response is developed for the new situation it must take into account all the subtasks that are affected. The information collection and problem solving activities may be substantial. To handle this task new roles are created, called managerial roles, and arranged in a hierarchy as shown in Figure 3.[2] The occupants of these roles handle the information collection and decision making tasks necessitated by uncertainty.

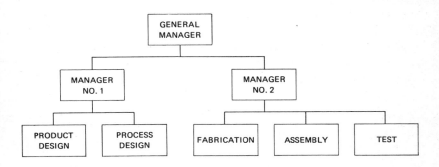

Fig. 3 Hierarchical organization structure.

Then as unanticipated events arise, the problem is referred to the manager who has the information to make a new decision. In addition, the hierarchy is also a hierarchy of authority and reward power, so that the decisions of the role occupants are effective determinants of the behavior of the task performers. In this manner the hierarchy of authority is employed on an exception basis. That is, the new situation, for which there is no preplanned response, is referred upward in the hierarchy to permit the creation of a new response. Since the process we are describing remains rather mechanical, the new situation is referred upward in the hierarchy to that point where a shared superior exists for all subunits affected by the new situation. For example, in Figure 3, if a problem arises during testing which requires product design work, it is referred to the general manager. If a situation arises affecting assembly and fabrication, it is referred to manager No. 2.

It is important to point out that the hierarchy is employed *in addition to, not instead of,* the use of rules. That is, the rules achieve coordination for the uniform and repetitive situations, whereas the new and unique situations are referred upward. This combination guarantees an integrated coordinated organizational response to the situations which the organization faces.

The weakness of hierarchical communication systems is that each link has a finite capacity for handling information. As the organization's subtasks increase in uncertainty, more exceptions arise which must be referred upward in the hierarchy. As more exceptions are referred upward, the hierarchy becomes overloaded. Serious delays develop between the upward transmission of information about new situations and a response to that information downward. In this situation, the organization must develop new processes to supplement rules and hierarchy.

Targeting or Goal Setting

As task uncertainty increases, the volume of information from the points of action to points of decision making overload the hierarchy. In this situation it becomes more efficient to bring the points of decision down to the points of action where the information originates. This can be accomplished by increasing the amount of discretion exercised by employees at lower levels of the organization. However, as the amount of discretion exercised at lower levels of the organization is increased, the organization faces a potential behavior control problem. That is, how can the organization be sure that the employees will consistently choose the appropriate response to the job-related situations which they will face?

In order to increase the probability that employees will select the appropriate behavior, organizations make two responses to deal with the behavior control problem.[3] The first change involves the substitution of craft or professional training of the work force for the detailed centralized programming of the work processes.[4] This is illustrated by a comparison between manufacturing industries and construction industries. In mass production, the work processes that are planned in advance are:

1) the location at which a particular task will be performed

2) the movement of tools, of materials and of workers to this work place and the most efficient arrangement of these workplace characteristics
3) sometimes the particular movements to be performed in getting the task done
4) the schedules and time allotments for particular operations
5) inspection criteria for particular operations.

In construction all these characteristics of the work process are governed by the worker in accordance with the empirical lore that makes up craft principles.[5]

These two descriptions represent a shift from control based on supervision and surveillance to control based on selection of responsible workers. Workers who have the appropriate skills and attitudes are selected.

Professionalization by itself may not be sufficient to shift decision making to lower levels of the organization. The reason is that in the presence of interdependence, an alternative which is based on professional or craft standards may not be best for the whole organization. Thus alternatives which are preferred from a local or departmental perspective may not be preferred from a global perspective. The product design that is technically preferred may not be preferred by the customer, may be costly to produce, or may require a schedule which takes too long to complete. In order to deal with the problem, organizations undertake processes to set goals or targets to cover the primary interdependencies.

An example of the way goals are used can be demonstrated by considering the design group responsible for an aircraft wing structure. The group's interdependence with other design groups is handled by technical specifications elaborating the points of attachment of the wing to the body, forces transmitted at these points, centers of gravity, etc. The group also has a set of targets (not to be exceeded) for weight, design man-hours to be used, and a completion date. They are given minimum stress specifications below which they cannot design. The group then designs the structures and assemblies which combine to form the wing. They need not communicate with any other design group on work related matters if they and the interdependent groups are able to operate within the planned targets.

Thus goal setting helps coordinate interdependent subtasks and still allows discretion at the local subtask level. Instead of specifying specific behaviors through rules and programs, the organization specifies targets to be achieved and allows the employees to select behaviors appropriate to the target.[6]

The ability of the design groups to operate within the planned targets, however, depends partly on the degree of task uncertainty. If the task is one that has been performed before, the estimates of man-hours, weight, due date, etc., will probably be realized. If it is a new design involving new materials, the estimates will probably be wrong. The targets will have to be set and reset throughout the design effort.

The violation of planned targets usually requires additional decision making and hence additional information processing. The additional information processing takes place through the hierarchy in the same way that rule exceptions were handled. Problems are handled on an exception basis. They are raised to higher levels of the hierarchy for resolution. The problem rises to the first level at which a shared superior exists for all affected subunits. A decision is made, and the new targets are communicated to the subunits. In this manner the behavior of the interdependent subunits remains integrated.

However, as the organization performs more uncertain tasks, such as designing and building a 747 jumbo jet, the hierarchical channels become overloaded once again. The organization does not have the information to estimate how many man-hours are needed to design the new titanium wings. How much weight will the wings require? Will it take 9 months, a year, or 18 months to complete the design? The information necessary to make these decisions can only be discovered during the actual design. The decisions must be made and remade each time new information is discovered. The volume of information processing can overwhelm an organization behaving in the mechanical fashion outlined in this chapter. The organization must adopt a strategy to either reduce the information necessary to coordinate its activities or increase its capacity to process more information. In the next section these strategies are identified and integrated into the framework. Subsequent chapters explain the strategies in detail.

DESIGN STRATEGIES

The ability of an organization to successfully coordinate its activities by goal setting, hierarchy, and rules depends on the combination of the frequency of exceptions and the capacity of the hierarchy to handle them.

As task uncertainty increases, the number of exceptions increases until the hierarchy is overloaded. Then the organization must employ new design strategies. Either it can act in two ways to reduce the amount of information that is processed, or it can act in two ways to increase its capacity to handle more information. An organization may choose to develop in both of these ways. The two methods for reducing the need for information and the two methods for increasing processing capacity are shown schematically in Figure 4. The effect of all these actions is to reduce the number of exceptional cases referred upward into the organization through hierarchical channels.

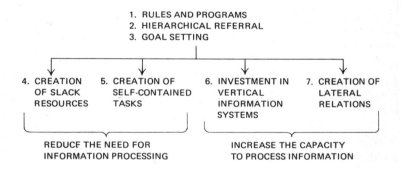

Fig. 4 Organization design strategies.

Creation of Slack Resources

An organization can reduce the number of exceptions that occur by simply reducing the required level of performance. In the example of the wing design, the scheduled time, weight allowance, or man-hours could be increased. In each case more resources could be consumed. These additional resources are called slack resources.[7]

Slack resources are an additional cost to the organization or the customer. However, the longer the scheduled time available, the lower the likelihood of a target being missed. The fewer the exceptions, the less the overload on the hierarchy. Thus the creation of slack resources, through reduced performance levels, reduces the amount of information that must be processed during task execution and prevents the overloading of hierarchical channels. Whether the organization chooses this strategy depends on the relative costs of the other three strategies for handling the overload.

Creation of Self-Contained Tasks

The second method for reducing the amount of information processed is to change from the functional task design to one in which each group has all the resources it needs to perform its task. In the example of the 747, self-contained units could be created around major sections of the aircraft—wing, cabin, tail, body, etc. Each group would have its own product engineers, process engineers, fabricating and assembly operations, and test facilities. In other situations, groups can be created around product lines, geographical areas, projects, client groups, markets, etc., each of which would contain the input resources necessary for the task.

The strategy of self-containment shifts the basis of the authority structure from one based on input, resource, skill, or occupational categories, to one based on output or geographical categories. The shift reduces the amount of information processing through several mechanisms—two are described here.

First, it reduces the amount of output diversity faced by a single collection of resources. For example, a professional organization with multiple skill specialties that provides service to three different client groups must schedule the use of these specialties across three demands for their services and determine priorities when conflicts occur. But if the organization changes to three groups, one for each client category, each with its own full complement of specialties, the schedule conflicts across client groups disappears, and there is no need to process information to determine priorities.

The second source of information reduction occurs through a reduced division of labor. The functional or resource specialized structure pools the demand for skills across all output categories. In the example above, each client generates approximately one-third of the demand for each skill. Since the division of labor is determined by the extent of the market, the division of labor must decrease as the demand decreases. In the professional organization, each client group may have generated a need for one-third of a computer programmer. The functional organization would have hired one programmer and shared him across the groups. In the self-contained structure, there is insufficient demand in each group for a programmer, and so the professionals must do their own programming. Specialization is reduced but there is no problem of scheduling the programmer's time across the three possible uses for it.

Thus the first two strategies reduce overloads on the hierarchy by reducing the number of exceptions that occur. The reduction occurs by reducing the level of performance, diversity of output, or division of labor. According to the theory put forth earlier, reducing the level of performance, etc., reduces the amount of information required to coordinate resources in creating the organization's services or products. In this way, the amount of information to be acquired and processed during task execution, and as a consequence the amount of task uncertainty, is reduced.

In contrast, the other two strategies take the required level of information as given, and create processes and mechanisms to acquire and process information during task execution.

Investment in Vertical Information Systems

The organization can invest in mechanisms which allow it to process information acquired during task performance without overloading the hierarchical communication channels. The investment occurs according to the following logic. After the organization has created its plan or set of targets for weight, stress, budget, and schedule, unanticipated events occur which generate exceptions requiring adjustments to the original plan. At some point when the number of exceptions becomes substantial, it is preferable to generate a new plan rather than make incremental changes in the old one with each exception. The issue is then how frequently plans should be revised—yearly, quarterly, or monthly? The greater the uncertainty, the greater the frequency of replanning. The greater the frequency of replanning, the greater the resources, such as clerks, computer time, input-output devices, etc., required to process information about relevant factors.

Providing more information more often may simply overload the decision maker. Investment may be required to increase the capacity of the decision maker by employing computers, various man-machine combinations, assistants-to, etc. The cost of this strategy is the cost of information processing resources.

The investment strategy is to collect information at the points of origin and direct it, at appropriate times, to the appropriate places in the hierarchy. The strategy increases the information processing at planning time while reducing the number of exceptions which have overloaded the hierarchy.

Creation of Lateral Relations

The last strategy is to selectively employ lateral decision processes which cut across lines of authority. The strategy moves the level of decision making down to where the information exists rather than bringing it up to the points of decision. It decentralizes decisions but without creating self-contained groups. Several mechanisms are employed. The number and types depend upon the level of uncertainty.

The simplest form of lateral relation is direct contact between two people who share a problem. If a problem arises in testing (see Figure 3), the manager of test may contact the manager of assembly and secure the necessary change. Direct contact avoids the upward referral to another manager and removes overloads from the hierarchy.

In some cases there is a large volume of contact between two sub-tasks such as process design and assembly. Under these circumstances a new role, a liaison role, may be created to handle the interdepartmental contacts.

As tasks of higher uncertainty are encountered, problems are detected in testing which require the joint efforts of product and process design, assembly, and testing. Rather than refer the problem upwards, managers of these areas form a task force or team to jointly resolve the issue. In this manner interdepartmental group problem solving becomes a mechanism to decentralize decisions and reduce hierarchical overloads.

As more decisions and more decisions of consequence are made at lower levels of the organization through interdepartmental groups, problems of leadership arise. The response is the creation of a new role, an integrating role.[8] The function of the role is to represent the general manager in the interdepartmental decisions for a particular brand, product line, project, country, or geographical unit. These roles are called product managers in commercial firms, project managers in aerospace, and unit managers in hospitals.

After the role is created the issue is, how much and what kind of influence does the role occupant need in order to achieve integration for the project, unit, or product. Mechanisms from supporting information and budget control all the way to dual reporting relations and the matrix design are employed under various circumstances described in later chapters.

In summary, lateral relations permit the moving of decisions to lower levels of the organization and yet guarantee that all information is included in the process. The cost of the strategy is the greater amounts of managerial time that must be spent in group processes and the overhead expense of liaison and integrating roles.

Choice of Strategy

Four strategies have been briefly presented. The organization can choose to follow one or some combination of several if it chooses. It will choose that strategy which is least expensive in its environmental context.

It is important to note that the four strategies are hypothesized to be an exhaustive set of alternatives. That is, if the organization is faced with greater uncertainty, due to technological change, higher performance standards, increased competition, or diversified product line to reduce dependence, the amount of information processing is increased. *The organization must adopt at least one of the four strategies when faced with greater uncertainty.* If it does not consciously choose one of the four, then the first, reduced performance standards, will happen automatically. The task information requirements and the capacity of the organization to process information are always matched. If the organization does not consciously match them, reduced performance through budget overruns or schedule overruns will occur in order to bring about equality. Thus the organization should be planned and designed simultaneously with the planning of the strategy and resource allocations. But if the strategy involves introducing new products, entering new markets etc., then some provision for increased information must be made. Not to decide is to decide, and it is to decide upon slack resources as the only strategy for removing hierarchical overload.

SUMMARY

This chapter has introduced the basic theory upon which the remainder of the book will build. Starting from the observation that uncertainty appears to make a difference in type of organization structure, it was postulated that uncertainty increased the amount of information that must be processed during task execution. Therefore perceived variation in organization form was hypothesized to be variation in the capability of the organization to process information about events that could not be anticipated in advance.

Uncertainty was conceived as the relative difference in the amount of information required and the amount possessed by the organization. The amount required was a function of the output diversity, division of labor, and level of performance. In combination the task uncertainty, division of labor, diversity of output, and level of performance determine the amount of information that must be processed.

Next the basic, mechanistic, bureaucratic model was introduced along with explanations of its information processing capabilities. It was shown that hierarchical communication channels can coordinate large numbers of interdependent subtasks but have a limited capacity to remake decisions. In response four strategies were articulated which either reduced the amount of information or increased the capacity of the organization to process more information. The way to decrease information was to reduce the determinants of the amount of information: performance levels, diversity, and division of labor. The strategies to increase capacity were to invest in the formal, hierarchical information process and to introduce lateral decision processes. Each of these strategies has its effects and costs. Subsequent chapters will discuss each strategy in more detail. In addition, case studies will be presented which highlight the various choices.

NOTES

1. James G. March and Herbert A. Simon, *Organizations* (New York: John Wiley, 1958), pp. 142–150.
2. For a more detailed discussion of hierarchical arrangements, see James C. Emery, *Organizational Planning and Control Systems* (New York: Macmillan, 1969), pp. 11–12.
3. There are two aspects to this problem. First, individuals may choose behaviors which are ineffective because they do not have the information or knowledge to make a rational choice. This is the cognitive problem addressed here. The other aspect is that individuals may have goals which are different from organizational goals. Processes for dealing with this problem have been discussed already in this series. See Richard Beckhard, *Organization Development: Strategies and Models* (Reading, Mass.: Addison-Wesley, 1969), pp. 35–40.

4. Arthur Stinchcombe, "Bureaucratic and Craft Administration of Production: A Comparative Study," *Administrative Science Quarterly,* September 1959, pp. 168–187.
5. Ibid., p. 170.
6. Here again there are motivation questions. How difficult should the goals be? Should incentives be attached to them? Should the manager participate in setting them? See John Campbell, Marvin Dunette, Edward Lawler, III, and Karl Weick, Jr., *Managerial Behavior, Performance and Effectiveness* (New York: McGraw-Hill, 1970), Chapter 15.
7. James G. March and Herbert A. Simon, *Organizations* (New York: John Wiley, 1958); and Richard Cyert and James G. March, *A Behavioral Theory of the Firm* (Englewood Cliffs, N.J.: Prentice-Hall, 1963).
8. Paul Lawrence and Jay Lorsch, *Organization and Environment* (Boston: Division of Research, Harvard Business School, 1967), Chapter 3.

Chapter 3
INFORMATION REDUCTION STRATEGIES

The organization design strategies discussed in this chapter are those that reduce the amount of information that must be processed. In terms of the information processing theory presented in Chapter 2, the amount of information is reduced by reducing the level of performance, division of labor, or diversity of output. Information processing is reduced by the creation of slack resources and the creation of self-contained authority structures. Let us look at the effects and costs of each of these strategies.

ALTERNATIVE 1: CREATION OF SLACK RESOURCES

The concept of slack is one of the core concepts of Herbert Simon's cognitive limits theory of organization.[1] The concept is best illustrated by a practical example.

In the late 1950's and early 60's a good deal of research was devoted to finding a solution to the job shop scheduling problem.[2] This is a very complex combinatorial problem. For example, if there are five parts, each requiring work on a sequence of five different machines, then there are 25 billion possible ways to schedule the parts; theoretically, all these ways need to be evaluated prior to choosing the best one. Even this extremely simple problem would require computer time amounting to several centuries of 24-hour days. Research on job shop scheduling was directed, therefore, to operationalizing more efficient evaluation techniques, such as dynamic programming, integer-linear programming, and Monte Carlo simulation.[3] However, none of these produced any practically useful results for large problems.

Research interest then shifted to the use of artificial intelligence to evaluate schedules. The original interest in artificial intelligence came from attempts to write computer programs which played chess. One approach was to have a chess expert verbalize his thought process while playing a game. Then a computer program would duplicate the thought process. Since computers can manipulate symbols faster than the human brain and have larger and more accurate memories, the computer should play better chess than the human. The problems involved in this area have proved to be quite difficult. But it was within this context that the job shop problem was tackled. If the man who schedules the job shop could verbalize how he sequences jobs on machines, then a computer program could be written which would do it better. One researcher describes in the following way his experience at trying to discover the thought process used to solve the problem:

> To say that I did not succeed in this effort would be something of an understatement. If these trips accomplished anything, they convinced me that there was something about this problem that I did not quite understand. Since I now believe this to be an important point, I shall attempt to describe the source of my confusion.
>
> In all my plant visits, I arranged to spend most of my time with the man in the organization responsible for the detailed sequencing of production orders. This seemed sensible to me since this was the man who every day somehow dealt with the vast complexity of the job shop problem—this was the man who should be able to tell me what I needed to know.
>
> Upon meeting this gentleman, therefore, it was with considerable anticipation that I would say that I had come to discuss with him his very complicated job shop scheduling problem. Without exception he would look somewhat perplexed and ask, "What job shop scheduling problem?"
>
> Despite my explanations . . . he never could see my definition of his problem. He showed me records which indicated in great detail that he met virtually all his promised deliveries, and he showed me other

records which revealed his precise control of costs, but he never admitted any problem of scheduling.

Now, as I said, my inability to elicit any recognition of a scheduling problem from people who schedule discouraged me. But I can now report that I have found the explanation.

The job shop problem is not recognized by most factory schedulers because *for them,* in most cases, no scheduling problem exists. That is there is no scheduling problem for them because the organization which surrounds the schedulers reacts to protect them from strongly interdependent sequencing problems.[4]

Thus the sales department knows that the scheduler cannot solve the complex scheduling problem. As a result, they quote to customers delivery times which are sufficiently long that the complex scheduling problem does not arise. The organization can remain competitive because they compete with other job shops facing scheduling problems that are identically complex. Their competitive market interaction determines a standard delivery time the same way that it establishes a price. If all customers wanted shorter delivery times, the job shops could respond by hiring more labor and under-utilizing it or by working overtime to remove bottlenecks. Or they could buy more machines and incur a lower level of machine utilization. Other examples could be given, but the result in each case is the same. *The organization responds by increasing the resources available rather than by utilizing existing resources more efficiently.* It does this not because of poor management but because it does not have the information processing and computational capacity to deal with the coordination requirements of interdependence. Instead, it creates additional resources by reducing performance standards. These additional resources are called slack resources. The slack resource takes the form of additional time that the customer must wait, in-process inventory, under-utilized man-hours and machine time, higher costs, etc.

The quotation presented above was chosen because it illustrates several features of slack resources. First, it illustrates that slack can be functional. It is usually regarded as bad and as something of which we must rid ourselves. While it does have its costs, it can be less costly than other alternatives in allowing rational action in the face of complexity. Second, the example illustrates the fact we are seldom consciously aware of slack. It is so pervasive that most of us are not aware of it unless something happens to force us to look for it. But it can be increased or decreased just like any other policy variable. And finally the example illustrates how slack can reduce complexity so as to create problems that we are capable of solving. Let us look more precisely at the information processing effects and costs.

Information Processing Effects

For the job shop, the combination of task uncertainty, diversity of parts, division of labor in the form of different labor skills and machines, and the interdependence between them create an information processing problem which overwhelms the decision making apparatus. The increased delivery time both reduces the number of factors that must be considered simultaneously when making a decision and the likelihood that another decision will be required. The longer the delivery time, the higher the probability that the organization will complete the job on time. The more jobs that are completed on time, the fewer the number of exceptional cases requiring decision making. Thus the delivery time can be increased until the number of exceptions is within the capacity of the hierarchy to handle them. When exceptions do occur, fewer factors need to be considered simultaneously. The longer delivery times permit the creation of in-process inventories between machine centers. Therefore machine breakdowns, quality rejects, or any other type of schedule disruption are not instantaneously transmitted to other departments. Over short periods of time the department is independent of other departments and can act autonomously. This means the decision maker does not have to collect information about first and second order effects of his decision on the other departments. The inventory absorbs them.

Similar results can be obtained by changing other resource targets. For example, the group designing wings for the 747 could lengthen their due dates. The allowable weight or man-hours consumed could be increased. Allowable stress could be decreased. In each case, the probability of an exception and the complexity to be considered when an exception occurs is thereby reduced. The reduced performance standards increase the resources consumed in the design process. The additional resources are the slack resources.

The amount of slack required depends on the degree of task uncertainty. The less the organization knows about its task, the greater the reduction in performance that is required. The performance level must be reduced until the number of exceptions is within the capacity of the organization to process them.

Costs

Although every increase in a target resource can produce the same information processing effect, each will have a different cost depending on the context. Increased delivery time means that the customer must wait longer. In manufacturing organizations, increased lead times generate inventories which absorb capital which could be used in alternative investments. Increased budget has the obvious cost of more money or man-hours consumed in producing the product. Changes to weight, stress, or other design specifications reduce the worth of the item to the user. In each case there is a cost. The greater the uncertainty, the greater the cost. Whether slack is chosen as the policy with which to absorb increased uncertainty depends on the relative costs of the other three strategies.

ALTERNATIVE 2: CREATION OF SELF-CONTAINED TASKS

The second method of reducing the information load was explained earlier as a shift from a functional group, or input-based task design, to one in which each group handled a category of output and contained all major resources needed to provide that output. For example, many business firms pursuing strategies of product diversification developed problems with their functional organizations.[5] Many found that by creating self-contained product divisions many of the overload problems disappeared. Chandler's work describes the situation at Du Pont during this period. Sears, Roebuck decided on self-contained geographical divisions, as have many state university systems like those in California and New York. Some aerospace firms have created self-contained divisions around major projects. Regardless of the type of organization, there is an output task around which self-sufficient resource groups can be created.

Effects on Information Processing

Some of the effects of changing from a functional group system to self-contained groups were described in the previous chapter. First, the output diversity faced by a single collection of resources is reduced. Reduced diversity reduces the information processing needed to schedule and reschedule the demands for shared resources. The problem is eliminated by eliminating the sharing. Second, there is usually a reduction in the division of labor and therefore fewer distinctly different resources whose work needs to be coordinated and scheduled. Both of these effects mean that less information is required to coordinate work across interdependent, specialized resources and to set priorities across demands for scarce, shared resources.

A third effect of self-contained groups is that the point of decision is moved closer to the source of information. Exceptions have to travel through fewer levels before reaching a shared superior. Decisions can be made at lower levels, supported by only local information. The reason is that other departments are relatively less affected than under the functional group system, since few resources are shared and each task is more or less independent.

An important variable is the degree of self-containment of the group and thereby the degree of decentralization in the larger organization. No group is completely self-contained, or else it would not be part of the same organization. Therefore the variable is the degree of self-containment and, consequently, the degree of decentralization that is permitted. For example, if the services of 15 different specialties are required to produce an organization's product lines, then a choice must be made when product divisions are created as to which services will be contained in the divisions and which will remain centralized in the corporate office. In general, the greater the diversity of the outputs and the greater the task uncertainty, the greater the self-containment. If the outputs are moderately diverse and tasks moderately unpredictable, then perhaps 8 to 10 services will be allocated to the divisions. The staffs for finance, accounting, research and development, legal, and industrial relations may remain functional and centralized at corporate headquarters. Under extreme diversity and uncertainty, only the financial and legal may remain in corporate headquarters. This type of structure is usually labeled a "conglomerate." In order to complete our discussion of which functions remain centralized, the costs of the self-containment strategy need to be discussed.

Costs

The creation of self-contained units, like each of the four strategies, has its cost. The costs are basically those connected with a reduction of skill specialization. In the case of physical equipment, there is a loss of economies of scale. If a manufacturing organization is broken down into product divisions, then several smaller pieces of equipment must replace one large piece. It is always more expensive to buy several pieces of equipment than to buy one large piece of equipment of the same total capacity.

There are also costs associated with the decreased division of labor. In a functional engineering organization there can be two electrical engineers—one electromechanical and one electronics. If the structure is changed to two product groups, two electrical engineers are still needed but they will be required to generalize across electromechanical and electronics applications. (This assumes that more knowledge is required to generalize across disciplines than across products.) If a high level of expertise is necessary, the organization can maintain one electromechanical and one electronics engineer for each product group. But now there is duplication involved. Four engineers are required instead of two. Expertise is maintained by the use of slack resources in the form of two additional engineers. Another aspect is that functional or skill-based structures provide career paths for people who remain in the same occupational group. They are physically located together and interact with members of their own specialty. These features disappear or are reduced in the self-contained structure.

The above costs apply differentially to the individual subtasks or functions. Some functions such as R & D, finance, and fabricating operations have economies of scale in the form of specialized manpower, borrowing leverage, risk pooling, and physical processing equipment. These functions tend to remain centralized and separate from the more self-contained groups. Thus for a given level of diversity and uncertainty, the greater the economies of scale, the less the degree of self-containment. Serious problems develop if a function is critical to providing the output, and therefore should be a part of the self-contained group, but also possesses economies of scale, and therefore should be centralized. This case is best handled with lateral relations.

SUMMARY

This chapter has presented two design strategies for dealing with the uncertainty and diversity of an organization's tasks. In both cases the effect of the design action is to reduce the interdependence between subunits, thus reducing the amount of information that must be processed during execution of the task. *Slack resources* produce fewer deviations from planned goals and hence fewer exceptions requiring decisions. *Changes in the authority structure* (in the direction of self-contained units) bring about less resource sharing and fewer specialized resources to be shared and scheduled. Decisions are moved closer to the origin of information. Each of these strategies has its costs. The costs should be compared with the costs of strategies which increase the capacity to process information.

NOTES

1. James G. March and Herbert A. Simon, *Organizations* (New York: John Wiley, 1958); and Richard Cyert and James G. March, *A Behavioral Theory of the Firm* (Englewood Cliffs, N.J.: Prentice-Hall, 1963).
2. A job shop is a manufacturing facility in which all machines performing a similar process, such as drilling, grinding, cutting, etc., are placed in the same department. There may be 15 to 50 such machine centers in a shop. As orders arrive they must be loaded on available machine time and also must meet customer delivery requirements. An order requires various types and amounts of machine time in various sequences. There may be 500 to 3000 orders in the shop. The magnitude of scheduling 3000 orders across 50 machine centers is a formidable problem.
3. John F. Muth and Gerald Thompson (eds.), *Industrial Scheduling* (Englewood Cliffs, N.J.: Prentice-Hall, 1963).
4. William F. Pounds, "The Scheduling Environment," in Muth and Thompson, op. cit., pp. 7 and 8.
5. Alfred Chandler, *Strategy and Structure* (Cambridge, Mass.: MIT Press, 1962).

Chapter 4
ALTERNATIVE 3: INVESTMENT IN A VERTICAL INFORMATION SYSTEM

The investment of resources in a vertical information system is the third design strategy. This strategy increases the capacity of existing channels of communication, creates new channels, and introduces new decision mechanisms. It also increases the capacity of the organization to make use of information acquired during task execution. This chapter is primarily concerned with design choices involving computers and the new information technology.

The effect of investing in a vertical information system is the same as creating slack resources and self-contained tasks—there are fewer exceptions referred up the hierarchy. The critical factor limiting an organization's attainment of high levels of performance in the presence of division of labor, size, and diversity is its ability to communicate and make decisions about unique, nonroutine, consequential events which could not be anticipated in advance. While the result is the same, the nature of the design choices and their costs are quite different.

In this chapter, we first introduce the policy dimensions which might lead to a choice of a vertical information system. The dimensions are then combined into some prototype information systems. Empirical evidence supporting the theory is then reviewed. Finally, a brief case study is used to summarize the chapter.

30

DIMENSIONS OF THE VERTICAL INFORMATION SYSTEM

Before discussing policy changes, the policy variables need to be identified. Four variables are of interest.[1] They are:

1. *Decision frequency,* or *timing,* of information flows to and from the decision mechanism.

2. *The scope of the data base* available to the decision mechanism.

3. *The degree of formalization* of the information flows to and from the decision mechanism.

4. *The capacity of the decision mechanism* to process information and select the appropriate alternative.

Let us look at each of these dimensions individually.

Decision Frequency, or Timing

The first dimension that can be changed is the length of time between decisions. Although the length of time is a continuous variable, let us dichotomize it for ease of discussion and look at the extreme types of decision frequencies. At one extreme of the dichotomy is the *periodic* information flow. For example, the job shop may schedule its operations once a month. At that time the status of orders and machines is relayed to the decision mechanism. A new schedule is created and communicated to those who must effect it. The distinctive feature is the fixed interval between successive collections of data and/or making of decisions. The other extreme of the dichotomy is a continuous collection of information and the making of decisions whenever decisions need to be made.

The timing or frequency of the goal setting process affects the number of exceptions that are referred upward in the hierarchy. Every set of goals or plan begins to decay in usefulness immediately after it is created. For example, the schedule for the job shop begins to decay as unplanned events occur such as machine breakdowns, worker absenteeism, engineering design changes, quality control rejects, order cancellations, etc. These events cause exceptions which are referred upward. As the hierarchy gets overloaded it becomes more efficient to create a new plan than to make incremental changes to the old one. So as the uncertainty of the task increases, the interval between plans decreases. The shorter the interval between plans, the fewer the number of exceptions. There are fewer exceptions because most exceptions occur late in the planning cycle when the decay has been greatest. The reduction in exceptions is gained at the cost of more processing of information at planning time. For example, reduction of the planning cycle from one month to two weeks doubles the amount of information processed at planning time. More clerks and/or computer time are required. But this option may be cheaper than using slack or creating self-contained structures.

Scope of the Data Base

The second dimension is the scope of the data base available to the decision mechanism. The scope, like timing, is dichotomized into pure types. If the decision mechanism has access to information pertaining only to its immediate location, the data base is called *local*. On the other hand if the decision mechanism has access to information concerning the state of affairs in all resource groups and for all output categories, the data base is *global*. The scope of the data base available to the decision mechanism affects its ability to coordinate activities in one part of the organization with those in other parts of the organization. The decision alternative which appears best from a local perspective may not be best from a global one. Furthermore, it is possible that the summation of a series of local optima will add up to less than a global optimum when interdependence exists. This phenomenon has been termed suboptimization.[2] Therefore the greater the interdependence between subunits, the greater the need for a global data base.

Like other strategies, increasing the scope of the data base means an increase in cost. The costs are incurred by the creation of the new information channels that are needed to bring together in one decision mechanism all the information pertaining to an interdependent set of subunits. One of the ways in which a global data base is implemented is by creating new *direct* information channels to a position in the hierarchy which has the global goal orientation required to reach high quality decisions. This kind of global system avoids the sequential processing of the hierarchical channels and reduces filtering and delays. The cost is the resources utilized to maintain additional information channels.

It should be pointed out that taking information from its points of origin and collecting it into a global data base to be presented at a level high in the hierarchy is only one method of operationalizing this dimension. Bringing information up to points of decision has as its primary virtue the avoidance of the problem of behavior control. That is, if the information is presented to the manager responsible for all the units involved, he will probably choose the alternative that is best for the entire unit. However, the policy dimension is to increase the scope of the data base available to the decision mechanism independent of what it is or where in the hierarchy it is located. But if global data is presented to a manager of a subunit, will he choose the alternative which is in the best interest of the global entity, or will he choose what is best for his subunit? At this point, the organization is no longer limited by cognitive factors but by goal factors. The situation requires a global goal orientation to be brought down to lower levels. Global goal orientations can be created by using strategy 2 to employ self-contained, autonomous groups at low levels of the organization. Another way is to design global incentive and reward systems. And the third method is to employ lateral relations, which are discussed in the next chapter.

The reason for this apparent side discussion is that too often the expedient of avoiding the behavior control problem is chosen, and the decision mechanism is placed high in the hierarchy. The power of computers and their use in nonhierarchical, democratic organization designs is virtually unexplored. Once computers are employed, many of the cognitive limiting factors disappear or no longer limit effectiveness. Organizations become limited by motivation, cooperation, and conflict-resolving technologies.

Formalization

A third dimension of the information system is the degree of formality of the collection and reporting processes. The formalization of categories for collecting and reporting information creates a language with which members of the organization can communicate about events that the organization faces. The most obvious example is the accounting system, which every organization has.

The primary effect of the formalized languages is to permit the transmission of information with fewer symbols, thereby enabling the communication channels to carry more information.[3] The ability of an organization to coordinate diverse outputs across specialized resources depends critically upon having an efficient means of identifying all the outputs and recording changes in them in the face of uncertainty. For this monitoring, some formalization of language is necessary. Also, the resources consumed in reporting information more often and through new channels is probably proportional to the number of symbols transmitted. Therefore, for a given information content, the more formal the information system, the fewer the resources consumed in transmission.

Formalization also has its costs and limitations. First, staffs are required to design and maintain these languages. Systems analysts and cost accountants are expensive personnel to maintain. A second limitation is that not all information lends itself to being formalized. To the extent that activities are ambiguous and require qualitative rather than quantitative measures, they are difficult to formalize. Formalization is therefore limited to the type of uncertainty that it can handle. Uncertainty in which the organization is uncertain about what the variables are and how they are related do not lend themselves to formal languages. Unique, nonroutine events still require nonformal, usually verbal channels. It is the type of uncertainty, in which known factors may acquire unknown values, that can be effectively handled by formalization. When used by itself formalization is limited in its ability to reduce overloads. Providing more information does not always improve the situation unless there is a means to process it. More information may simply overload the decision mechanism.

Decision Mechanism

The fourth policy dimension is the capacity of the decision mechanism to process information and select an alternative course of action. As suggested above, providing more information more often and more efficiently may simply overload the decision mechanism. Therefore, the capacity of the decision mechanism must be expanded with respect to its timing, scope, and formalization. There are various types of mechanisms.

Several years ago there would have been no need for a section entitled "Decision Mechanism." The manager was the decision maker. The structure of organizations was determined by his capacity to handle the decision situations with which he was faced. The only way to improve decision making was to select managers who made better decisions than other managers. Since that time there have been two major thrusts for improving decision making. One from the behavioral sciences has operationalized the process of group decision making. The use of a group for a decision mechanism affects not only the quality of a decision but the motivation to implement it. The next chapter will discuss the choice of group mechanisms. The second thrust has come from the new information technology made possible by computers.

The use of machines to reach routine decisions is now well known.[4] The use of machines as decision mechanisms has been credited with substantial reductions in slack in manufacturing firms. It is also known that computers have had more limited use in the less structured problems at middle and top levels of management. This recognition has led to research on man-machine decision mechanisms. The division of labor results in the man concentrating on creating alternatives and evaluating consequences, while the computer performs manipulations on large volumes of quantitative data in order to compute consequences of alternatives.[5] More recently it has been recognized that in order to include all global data, both machine-readable and verbal, group-machine decision mechanisms are needed. The use of visual displays in joint decision making appears to hold significant promise.[6] Figure 5 ranks the possible decision mechanisms in order of increasing capacity to process information and make decisions and also in order of increasing cost.

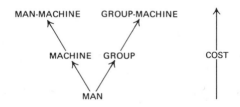

Fig. 5 Decision mechanisms.

PROTOTYPE INFORMATION SYSTEMS

The policy variables that must be considered in designing an information system can be combined into various prototype systems. The primary variables to be considered here are timing of decision making and scope of the data base, as depicted schematically in Figure 6. The systems will be discussed in sequence of increasing cost. A more costly system is required when an organization is faced with greater task uncertainty and greater task interdependence.

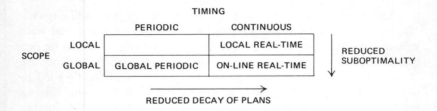

Fig. 6 Typology of information systems.

Local-Periodic System

The first logical system is the local periodic, which is not used extensively. It can be illustrated by the warehouse clerk who places orders every Friday to replenish his inventory. He places orders for those items whose actual stock level has fallen below a pre-set minimum level. The ordering is periodic and based only on local information available to the clerk. The system ignores interdependence. If a work center at the plant has a low work load, the clerk will not place an order to utilize that capacity because of the limited scope of the data available to him. In addition, if an unforeseen increase in demand occurs, the warehouse will stock-out and not be replenished until the next Friday. So while the system is simple and inexpensive, it ignores interdependence and is not responsive to uncertain environments.

Local Real-Time System

The second type of information system is the local real-time. It involves largely informal data collection on a continuous basis at the local level and man-dominated decision making. The decision making differs from that used in the local-periodic system in that decisions are made whenever a decision needs to be made. This system is best illustrated by the sequencing decision in job shops. The decision concerns the choice of which one of a number of waiting jobs should be processed next on an available machine. The decision is made by either the foreman or a dispatcher at the moment a machine becomes available. Therefore the decision is made in light of the most current information concerning the status of the department. This allows a last-minute matching of job, machine, and man to permit the most efficient functioning of the department. Many of the prevailing conditions may not have been predictable in advance. The current data base allows a responsiveness to uncertain environments.

The system has the defect, however, of a local data base. For example, the dispatcher may choose to load on a machine an order which appears best from the department's viewpoint. However, the order goes next to a machine center experiencing a machine breakdown, whereas another order could have gone to a machine center experiencing a temporary underload. A more global data base would prevent this accentuation of load discrepancies.

The virtue of the system is that it is inexpensive to sustain. Prior to the use of computers, such a system was the primary way to respond to task uncertainty. The interdependencies were handled by reducing their impact through the use of slack resources and selfcontained authority structures which eliminated the need for global data.

Global-Periodic System

The third information and decision system is the global-periodic structure. This structure has also been applied to the scheduling of job shops. A typical process would begin by collecting information about the status of completion of all orders in all machine centers. This information would be fed into a computer. The computer would be equipped with a simulation program or similar algorithm to compute start dates for all jobs on all machines. The program would be written so as to meet the promised delivery dates and keep the machine centers loaded. These new start dates would be transmitted to all foremen and would be the basis for loading machines for a period of one week. At the end of the week the process would be repeated.

Such a system is characterized by formalized information collection and machine-aided decision making, which are necessary in order to expand the capacity of the information channel and the decision mechanism to handle the larger volumes of data. This type of structure is typical of batch processing computer systems.

Global-periodic structures vary in application in two ways—the nature of the review period and the comprehensiveness of the plan. The review period can be either fixed or variable. In the example above it was fixed and the interval was one week. While variable lengths are possible, review periods are almost always fixed, with the interval length being a design variable. There are several reasons for desiring a fixed interval for review. First, there is a desire for predictability and regularity in the usage of batch processing computers. Second, a fixed interval allows the making of a number of decisions simultaneously which affect a number of departments. For example, the decisions can be made simultaneously for production labor capacity and personnel hiring. Finally, we do not know when conditions have changed sufficiently to remake a decision. Instead we fix an interval whose length approximates the needs for adaptation on the average.

A plan is comprehensive to the extent that the decision process considers the bulk of the economically and physically relevant variables. The job shop schedule is comprehensive to the extent that it considers limited machine capacities, technically feasible machine substitutes to smooth work loads, the possibility for splitting orders to reduce a bottleneck, etc. Such comprehensiveness requires formalization and computerization to handle the large volumes of data needed to support the decision. Since this is expensive, organizations vary in the comprehensiveness of their plans. Those factors not considered in the global plan are either ignored or left to be resolved at the local level.

The global-periodic structure has characteristics opposite to those of the local real-time system. By simultaneously determining schedules for all orders, it takes full account of the interdependencies between departments. In addition, the computational power of the computer is exploited. The result is a schedule which is best from the point of view of the organization, not a schedule which is the summation of the best decisions from each department. However, the schedule is subject to the decay process mentioned earlier. After it is put into effect on Monday morning, the series of machine breakdowns, quality rejects, and engineering changes may render the schedule ineffective by Wednesday. Thus the global data base and computational power reduce suboptimal decision making, but the periodicity subjects the decisions to decay.

The global-periodic structure has been used extensively in applications with low to moderate uncertainty. The applications have exploited the power of the computer and the global data. The decay process in these applications is a minor irritant, not a major disadvantage. Most of the research into this structure and some of the speculation have been the result of observations of changes from local real-time to global-periodic structures. Let us look at the results from the most comprehensive study available.[7]

Whisler has made a study of 23 insurance companies. This industry has made extensive use of computers for a long period of time. The applications studied were almost all concerned with batch processing computers. The changes have been from local real-time to global-periodic structures. The following organization changes have resulted.

1. *Reduced Personnel.*   There is usually an impact on the *configuration* of the organization in the form of fewer clerical personnel. This is usually difficult to measure because the firms grow during implementation and also take on new activities. The best indicator is the estimated number of additional personnel that would be needed to perform current activities without computers. They are:

Clerical 60%
Supervisory 9%
Managerial 2%

These data show both the magnitude and location of the effect. Computers have had their greatest impact at the routine, operating level of organizations.

2. *Integration and Consolidation of Subtasks.*   In addition to reduced numbers of clerks, the most ubiquitous phenomenon was integration of subtasks or increasing interdependence.

> Without exception, the companies in this study reported that computer applications have consolidated or will soon consolidate decision making areas that were previously separate. In no case has the reverse effect occurred, they say . . . computer systems reverse the effects of organizational growth and development, restoring fragmented decision systems to the state of integration that would have been logically and economically desirable had it not been for acute problems of information overload.[8]

This increased interdependence was coordinated in various ways. The organizations seem to have choosen different design strategies. Let us see the overall results before speculating.

3. *Reorganization from Self-Contained Departments into Functional Departments.* Integrating subtasks usually was accompanied by organizational consolidation of the departments responsible for the subtasks. The use of the computer in the decision process reduced the information overload and allowed a functional organizational structure to operate efficiently. For example, one company regrouped its two self-contained accounting departments into two functional departments as follows:[9]

Before Computer	*After Computer*
Premium and commission (first-year policies)	Commission accounting (all policies)
Accounting (first-year policies)	Premium accounting (all policies)
Premium and commission (renewed policies)	
Accounting (renewed policies)	

These changes permit greater specialization of skills due to the larger functional groups. The computer permits the coordination of the specialized units.

Not all the organizations changed to functional structures. Those who had had the systems installed the longest and who were growing at slower rates changed to functional structures. The organizations dealing with greater uncertainty maintained self-contained structures or, as we shall see shortly, achieved global decision structures without changing the formal authority structure.

4. *Centralization of Decision Making.* Most of the organizations reported that control was centralized or that choices were made at higher levels of the organization. These changes are consistent with the change to a functional organization and an increase in subtask interdependence. An exception now had an impact on more departments and was more consequential. In addition, many decisions were programmed into the computer. There was greater rationalization and quantification of decisions in many organizations.

All these four findings fit together. The increase in interdependence, the increase in information processing capacity, the change to a functional organization, centralization of decisions, and quantification appear as parts of one total strategy.

5. *More Group Decision Making.*   Several organizations indicated that tying together subtasks need not result in consolidating under a single authority those units that perform the work. Coordination takes place by using the strategy described in the next chapter—group decisions.

> On the other hand, one of the greatest benefits of computer automation, in my opinion, has been the development of group decision making as a staff function rather than hierarchical decision making through line relationships. The unifying relationship in these varying groups assembled for decision making usually is either a consolidated record file (i.e., personnel and payroll functions joined procedurally through a common master record but separate organizationally) or a series of separate record files that are joined together procedurally in a continuous computer operation with input and output cutting across existing organizational lines.
>
> The trend toward group decision making has evolved largely on a voluntary basis, I believe. What probably began as a "getting together" for the purpose of coordination and communication has subtly evolved into something more like "consensus decision making." Generally, however, the person upon whom the responsibility for a decision would be expected to fall, from an organizational standpoint, would be considered by the group as having actually made the final decision. This, again, points up the increasingly complex line-and-staff relationships now involved in decision making in highly computer-oriented organizations.[10]

These findings support the theory being developed in this book. The use of computers in the modification of the vertical information system is an alternative to the creation of self-contained structures in handling information overloads.

The increase in group decision making suggests that computers need not lead to centralized, functional structures. With a sample size of 23, Whisler had limited opportunity for multivariate analysis, but it is probable that group decision making is an alternative to centralization, as was suggested earlier. The least centralized organizations are probably those using group decisions. All these factors suggest alternative structures for exploiting the advantages of computers and global data bases.

On-Line, Real-Time

The last prototype would logically be the global-continuous structure, but in the current vernacular it is known as on-line real-time. It is characterized by the continuous flow of formalized global data and man-machine involvement in decision making. The best examples of such systems are airline reservation systems and Ticketron systems for sporting and theater events. These systems allow rapid updating of a constantly changing status and make the information available everywhere.

The on-line real-time structure is perfect in theory. It permits inter-unit consistency of action and reduces decay of plans by responding to new situations. In addition, when using remote-access computer terminals, the computational power of the computer can be brought to bear at the moment of decision and at the convenience of the manager.

On-line real-time structures have two problems. First, the remote-access and time-shared computers are very expensive to acquire and maintain. The second problem is our inability to create new organization structures to fully utilize the computers. The cultural lag is very evident here. We cannot foresee the ramifications of information instantaneously available everywhere in the organization. Information is a source of power, and so the present power structure is threatened. Most of our attitudes and behaviors still reflect hierarchical and sequential processing of data.

Despite these costs, there are some systems now in use which approximate the prototype structure. Two job shops have implemented systems which utilize global data and provide updates every one and three days respectively.[11] The result is a reduction of slack time. Average lead times to complete work were reduced 20 to 30 percent. Once again we see the trade-off of design strategies—vertical information system vs. slack resources.

EXAMPLES OF INFORMATION SYSTEMS

The research reviewed earlier in this book leads to the conclusion that there is no one best way to organize. Similarly there is no one best information system. This conclusion can be illustrated by a comparative study of three multispecialist medical clinics.[12]

The clinics allow patients to see a number of specialists rather than a single general practitioner. A typical clinic might have five to six specialists in each of ten to twelve departments. There are usually three or four laboratories and x-ray facilities. These specialized resources, both doctors and equipment, are expensive. Therefore, it is important to achieve full utilization of their time. A scheduling problem arises because each patient must usually see a number of doctors. The specialization causes interdependence. The scheduling is difficult because there is considerable uncertainty as to which doctors a patient should see, in which order, and for how long. In order to schedule a patient, a diagnosis is needed before he or she arrives. For returning or referred patients, this is available, but not for new ones.

Rockart has attempted to design a scheduling system for one clinic, based on a comparative study of several other clinics. The first clinic operates on a local real-time basis. The patients arrive, are examined by a doctor, and are routed to other doctors on the basis of the examination. There is no detailed prescheduling. The diagnosis is made and the schedule determined after all the facts are in. Moreover, the schedule is based on local information. In order to prevent schedule conflicts and underutilized doctors, this clinic uses slack time. The situation is analogous to the job shop. Instead of parts flowing through machine centers, patients flow through medical departments. The waiting lines guarantee full utilization of doctors and equipment. The cost is that the patient spends a good deal of his time waiting. This cost is minimized in a way because patients travel to this clinic, which is located in a rural setting. Patients arrange their affairs so as to have time available. While they are at the clinic there are few competing uses of their time and they have the expectation of a relaxing wait.

The other two clinics have a more difficult problem. They are located in large metropolitan areas. Their patients do not like to wait, since they have alternative uses for their time. Hotel accommodations are expensive. So these clinics must find a way to keep doctors fully utilized without long delays to patients.

Any solution must accept the level of specialization as given. Since slack resources cannot be used, the clinics must either reduce uncertainty or devote more resources to coordination. One clinic is trying the first strategy by sending an elaborate questionnaire to new in-coming patients in order to discover symptoms, perform a diagnosis, and schedule the appropriate doctors. Success would allow a global-periodic scheduling procedure.

The last clinic studied by Rockart used a global-periodic structure but without reducing uncertainty. A central, twenty-man staff received incoming phone calls and mail and tried to schedule the requests on global listings of doctor availability. However, the decay process was significant and doctors averaged fifteen minutes a day of idle time and patients waited thirty minutes per appointment. The decay was caused by patients who failed to show up, doctors who were called away, changes in doctor assignments, etc. To adapt to this situation Rockart designed an on-line real-time system to allow global data to be used in scheduling patients through multiple doctors without a significant decay process invalidating the schedule. It can now be updated rapidly and rescheduling can take place as needed. This structure increases costs by about $75,000 a year, but it permits specialization.

Our discussion illustrates quite clearly the two points of emphasis. First, there is no one best information system. The clinics mentioned above operate identical technologies with different information systems, yet all are effective organizations. The second point is that the information system is only one of several organization design variables. In this case the basis of departmentalization is fixed, and it is the task uncertainty, slack, and information systems that must be combined into a consistent system. The rural clinic is able to operate under high uncertainty and a simple information system by using slack time. The second clinic is attempting to reduce uncertainty to permit a global-periodic information system and thereby reduce slack time. This may be done also by operating only from referrals. The third clinic accepted the high uncertainty and is trying to reduce slack time with an on-line real-time scheduling information system. All these combinations are internally consistent and can lead to effective operations.

SUMMARY

This chapter has discussed the use of the new information technology as an organization design strategy. As with the previous strategies, we have discussed the effects on information overload. The controllable design attributes were identified and cast into various prototype information systems. Effects and costs were discussed. Empirical studies highlighted the nature of the alternative strategies in existing organizations.

NOTES

1. This framework comes from the work of Donald C. Carroll, "On the Structure of Operational Control Systems," in John Pierce (ed.), *Operations Research and the Design of Management Information Systems* (New York: Technical Association of the Pulp and Paper Industry, 1967), pp. 391–415.
2. Charles Hitch, "Suboptimization in Operations Problems," *Journal of the Operations Research Society,* May 1953, pp. 87–99.
3. James G. March and Herbert A. Simon, *Organizations* (New York: John Wiley, 1958), pp. 161–166.
4. Herbert A. Simon, *The New Science of Management Decision* (New York: Harper and Row, 1960).
5. See Donald C. Carroll, "Man-Machine Cooperation on Planning and Control Problems," *Industrial Management Review,* Fall 1966, pp. 47–54.
6. Michael S. Scott-Morton, "Management Decision Systems" (Boston: Division of Research, Harvard Business School, 1971).
7. Thomas L. Whisler, *The Impact of Computers on Organizations* (New York: Praeger Publishers, 1970).
8. *Ibid.,* p. 60.
9. *Ibid.,* pp. 62, 72.
10. *Ibid.,* p. 74.
11. Elwood Buffa, *Production-Inventory Systems* (Homewood, Ill.: Richard D. Irwin, 1968), Chapter 12.
12. John Rockart, "Scheduling in Multi-Specialist Group Medical Practice" (Cambridge, Mass.: M.I.T., 1967), unpublished Ph.D. dissertation.

Chapter 5
ALTERNATIVE 4: CREATION OF LATERAL RELATIONS

The final organization design strategy is to employ lateral forms of communication and joint decision making processes. That is, instead of referring a problem upward in the hierarchy, the managers solve the problem at their own level, contacting and cooperating with peers in those departments affected by new information. In this chapter, lateral forms of direct contact, liaison departments, task forces, and teams are discussed. A case study illustrating the design and use of these processes follows in Chapter 6.

LATERAL PROCESSES

As with the other design strategies, the purpose is to reduce the number of decisions being referred upward. As with vertical information systems, the effect is to increase the capacity of the organization to process information and make decisions. Lateral relations accomplish this by increasing discretion at lower levels of the organization, in contrast to some computer applications which transmit information from points of origin to a central decision point to exploit global information. Such computerized information systems are effective when the decision in question requires formalized, quantitative data. However, if the information relevant to a particular decision is qualitative, it is more effective to bring the point of decision down to the points where the information originated. Lateral processes should also be contrasted with the creation of self-contained groups. This strategy also increased discretion at lower levels of the organization. Discretion was possible at a low level because there was little sharing of resources across groups. A group did not need information about another group when solving a problem. However, if discretion is to be increased at lower levels without reducing resource sharing, lateral relations are required. They are necessary in order to acquire all the information relevant to the shared resources and the possible uses of shared resources.

Some of the forms of lateral relations make use of what is referred to as the "informal organization," or cliques.[0] These informal processes are thought to arise spontaneously and are the processes through which most organizations accomplish their work despite the formally designed structure. A typical point of view is, "If we had to go through channels, we would never get anything done." The point of view being taken here is that these informal processes are necessary as well as inevitable, but their use can be substantially improved by designing them into the formal organization. At the very least, organizations can be designed so as not to prevent these processes from arising spontaneously, and reward systems can be designed to encourage such processes.[1] But a more important reason for formalization is that these processes do not always arise spontaneously from the task requirements, especially in highly differentiated organizations. When the relevant participants have different and sometimes antagonistic attitudes, come from different countries, and are separated geographically, the effective use of joint decision making requires formally designed processes.

There are several forms of lateral relations. Some are simple, obvious, and inexpensive. Others are more sophisticated, costly and require more design attention. The forms are listed below in order of increasing cost. It is hypothesized that in order to be effective, organizations will utilize these forms in proportion to the amount of task uncertainty. Thus as task uncertainty increases, the organization will sequentially adopt these mechanisms up through the matrix organization. The forms are also cumulative, in the sense that higher forms are added to, not substituted for, lower forms.

1. Utilize *direct contact* between managers who share a problem.

2. Establish *liaison roles* to link two departments which have substantial contact.

3. Create temporary groups called *task forces* to solve problems affecting several departments.

4. Employ groups or *teams* on permanent basis for constantly recurring interdepartmental problems.

5. Create a new role, an *integrating role,* when leadership of lateral processes becomes a problem.

6. Shift from an integrating role to a *linking-managerial role* when faced with substantial differentiation.

7. Establish dual authority relations at critical points to create the *matrix design.*

The first four of these relations are discussed in this chapter.

Direct Contact

The simplest and least costly form of lateral relationship is direct contact between managers jointly affected by a problem. For example, in Figure 7, suppose that department A is about to overrun its schedule on an item which goes next to department D. In a vertical information system, the problem would be referred upward to G for resolution. But with direct contact, the manager of A can contact D directly and they can reach a

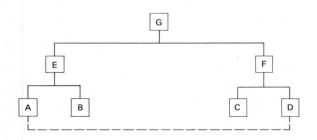

Fig. 7 Hierarchy utilizing direct contact.

mutually agreeable joint decision. If problems can be resolved in this manner, the number of exceptions flowing up and down the hierarchy is reduced. The top managers are then left free for those decisions that cannot be solved by direct contact between lower-level managers.

From an information processing view, direct contact relieves overloads by moving decisions from high in the hierarchy to lower levels. Such contact should improve the quality of the decision making because managers A and D have more information relevant to the decision. However, A and D may reach a decision which is not in the best interest of the organization as a whole. To insure good decisions, the organization should have a reward system which rewards cooperative behaviors,[2] managers who are interpersonally competent, norms which make such collaboration legitimate, and clearly visible departmental targets. If these supporting factors are not present, they should become the objectives for organization development activities.

There is another way to improve these informal practices. Many organizations engage in the practice of laterally transferring personnel from one department to another. This practice is usually part of the management development program. If an individual has a series of experiences in specialist departments, then he is prepared for a general management position. The effects of such transfers on attitudes and communication behavior have been tested.[3] The findings clearly indicate that managers having interdepartmental experience communicate laterally to a larger number of colleague managers than managers not having interdepartmental experience. Similar findings were reported for a Japanese R & D organization.[4] In the second study it was discovered that the effects of the transfer diminish with time. People transferred ten years ago behave the same way as individuals who have had no experience.

A second finding is that individuals with interdepartmental experience use more informal means to communicate when engaging in a lateral contact. They will use a telephone call, a face-to-face contact, or an informal meeting. Those not having the experience are more likely to use a memo. Therefore the transfer increases the probability that the individual will engage in a problem-solving dialogue rather than use a less effective one-way medium of communication.

The last finding is that managers with interdepartmental experience tend to establish reciprocal relations. That is, they receive as many contacts as they initiate, and therefore are less likely to be always pushing someone or to be always pushed by others. Most satisfying relationships are reciprocal.

The lateral transfer apparently improves lateral relations by reducing the impersonality of the contact. Managers with interdepartmental experience have the same attitudes toward their goals as managers without the experience. They pursue parochial departmental goals to the same degree as other managers. However, they are more likely to perceive the presence of conflict. This may be why they choose a more personal approach to the contact. In addition, no one likes to call a department. It is far preferable to call a person. If one calls a department he is likely to get low-level personnel and a predictable, rule-oriented response. It is difficult to ask people you do not know for favors. However, if you know that Paul works in the department, he may not be able to help you but can set you up with someone else who can. This is why the transfer effect decays over time. The promotion, transfer, and turnover process causes a loss of personal contacts.

Therefore, it appears that lateral transfers result in more lateral contacts and more effective contacts. In addition the organization gets something for nothing if it already uses lateral transfers. The only thing needed is to transfer personnel between interdependent departments and to transfer often enough to offset the diminishing time effect. If transfers are not used currently, they should be evaluated against the costs of lost specialization and lost productivity due to learning time.

Liaison Roles

When the volume of contacts between any two departments grows, it becomes economical to set up a specialized role to handle communication between them. Liaison men are typical examples of specialized roles designed to facilitate communication between two interdependent departments and to bypass the long lines of communication involved in upward referral.

The best example of this role is the engineering liaison man in a manufacturing plant. He is part of the engineering organization but is physically located in the plant to serve the production organization. These roles link two functional departments at low levels of the organization.

Task Forces

Direct contact and liaison roles, like the integration mechanisms discussed before, have a limited range of usefulness. They work when two managers or functions are involved. When problems arise involving seven or eight departments, direct contacts are not sufficient to reach a joint decision. These problems are usually referred upward. For uncertain, interdependent tasks, such situations arise frequently.

Task forces are a form of horizontal contact designed for problems of multiple departments. The task force is made up of representatives from each of the affected departments. Some are full-time members; others may be part-time. The task force is a temporary group. It exists only as long as the problem remains. When a solution is reached each participant returns to his normal tasks.

To the extent that they are successful, task forces remove problems from higher levels of the hierarchy. The decisions are made at lower levels in the organization. In order to guarantee integration, a group problem-solving approach can be taken. Each affected subunit contributes a member who provides information necessary for the task force and is able to judge the impact of its decisions on the home unit.

These groups may arise informally or on a formal basis. In one company, when a problem arises on the assembly floor the foreman calls the process engineer, a member from the company laboratory, quality control, and purchasing if vendor parts are involved. This group works out the problem. When an acceptable solution is created, they return to their normal duties.

On other occasions, the establishment of the group is more formal. An aerospace firm holds weekly design reviews. When a significant problem arises, a group is appointed, given a deadline, a limit to their discretion, and asked to solve the problem. Quite frequently the functional hierarchies of manufacturing firms are supported by task forces to introduce new products or processes. The task force is a temporary patchwork on the functional structure, used to short-circuit communication lines in a time of high uncertainty. When the uncertainty decreases, the functional hierarchy resumes its guiding influence.

Teams

As tasks become less predictable, more problems arise during execution. At some point, the combined use of rules, plans, direct contact, task forces, and upward referral may no longer be adequate to the task of maintaining integration. If the delays in decisions become long, lines of communication become extended, and top managers are forced to spend more time on day-to-day operations, the next response is to use group

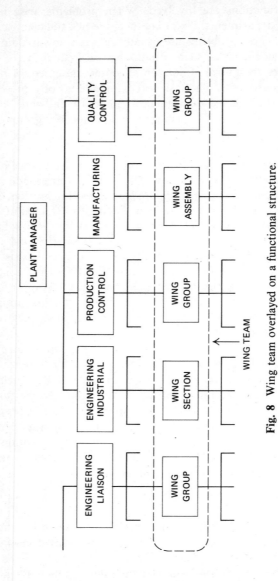

Fig. 8 Wing team overlayed on a functional structure.

problem solving on a more permanent basis. Teams are typically formed around frequently occurring problems. Such teams can meet daily or weekly to discuss problems affecting the group. They solve all the problems which require commitments that they are capable of making. Larger problems are referred upward.

Teams can be formed at various levels. Actually an entire hierarchy of teams can be designed. The design of team structures presents the same kind of departmentalization problems that are involved in the design of the formal hierarchy of authority. They can be formed around common customers, clients, geographic regions, functions, processes, products, or projects. If the hierarchy of authority is based on common functions such as engineering, production, and marketing, the teams can be formed around products, with representatives from each function. Thus the teams involve design decisions concerning the basis of the team, the composition of membership, the levels at which they are to operate, the range of their discretion, and the frequency of their meetings. The interdependence pattern and the basis for the authority structure should determine the basis and composition of membership. In addition the greater the task uncertainty, the greater the number of levels at which teams should operate, the more frequent should be their meetings, and the greater should be the range of their discretion.

An interesting example of teams can be found in an aerospace firm's manufacturing operations. The formal authority structure is based on common functions, as illustrated in Figure 8. Teams were formed around the major sections of the aircraft that were being produced. In addition, the groups were physically located around common aircraft sections. All groups working on the wing were located in the same area of the plant. Thus the physical location facilitated the lateral communication process and team structure. The design was an attempt to achieve the benefits of both a functional form and a task or project form.

MAKING LATERAL PROCESSES EFFECTIVE

The use of group decision making in organizations is a topic that never fails to elicit strong opinions—pro and con. There are usually good reasons for these opinions. Good and bad examples of groups are readily available. However some learning has taken place from these good and bad experiences, so that something can be said about the situations in which groups are most and least effective. This section attempts to articulate the factors that must be changed in order for lateral relationships to "fit" into the mosaic of the organization's processes rather than work at cross purposes.

In addition there are some operational decisions which affect team effectiveness. Even if there is a supportive managerial climate, questions remain about representation. Who should participate in the team? Which functions? From what level in the organization? Should they be full-time or part-time team members? What kinds of people make the best members? Or does representation make any difference? Obviously the opinion expressed here is that these factors do make a difference. Let us look at those representational and climate factors which seem to make a difference.

1. *Perceived Reward and Importance.* The degree to which participants are willing to commit themselves to the group task depends on the degree to which the group's performance will be instrumental in satisfying their needs. This will depend on how important they perceive it to be, whether they believe they have the needed skills, and whether their performance in the group will be evaluated or taken into account at their performance review. These factors, despite their appearing to be obvious, account for a substantial proportion of the negative attitudes toward groups. Nor are they trivial issues to deal with. This fact can be demonstrated by some examples.

The use of lateral relations has been adopted by several government agencies. The thinking is that a new agency need not be formed for each new social problem. Existing agencies can cooperate by forming temporary task forces as problems arise and easily disband them as problems are solved. Their efforts have been less than successful for several reasons, but one is the perceived reward system. In one of the participating agencies not using Civil Service, a questionnaire was used to assess which activities were perceived by the managers as most likely lead to a promotion.[5] Out of twenty possible activities, participation in interagency projects was ranked last. Similar conditions prevail among university professors.[6] How do these conditions arise? How can they be changed so that the individual is willing to commit himself?

The individual's perception of task activity is a function of the process by which assignments are made to the task force. The assignment process is the mechanism by which superiors communicate their expectations about task importance. If participation is unimportant and therefore not part of the reward system, the superior will make assignments in a way that communicates that fact.

One approach is to assign the low performer. Since the task force is thought to be a waste of time, the boss will not want to waste any resources. Therefore the assignment goes to whomever can be spared. The astute employees get this message very quickly. In addition, it staffs the task force with those people who are most likely to make it fail.

A second approach is to assign people to take turns. Individuals are made to feel that it is their "turn in the barrel." This perception is expressed when the subordinate objects to an assignment on the basis that he is already very busy. The response of the superior is not to relieve him of previous tasks but to ask that he take on this other assignment because it is his turn. The department is expected to provide staff, and rotation is an equitable way to handle the assignment. Again the message is clear. It is also reinforced by other members of the group.

In order to change the reward system and assignment process, the attitudes of the assigning managers need to be changed. It may be pointed out to the managers that their assignment methods appear valid but that their behavior determined the outcome they expected—that is, low performance by the task force. Therefore the organization development effort must deal with the managers' attitudes toward group decision making. The managers must get to a point where they are willing to try to make it work. They are the ones who will assign competent participants, reward performance, relieve participants of previous assignments, and communicate importance. But these behaviors occur only if managers believe there is a reasonable chance that the task force will accomplish something. The O.D. educational effort must deal with the attitudes that bring about the self-fulfilling prophecy.

2. *Assignment of Line Managers.*   At least a substantial minority of the team or task force must consist of managers who will subsequently be held responsible for the implementation of the joint decision. If all the Department of Defense task force studies were separated into those that were implemented and those that were discarded, the discarded task force studies would be characterized by exclusive participation of staff groups and outside consultants. It is not that these groups are useless but that they lack the insight of the man who has the original problem and commitment from the man who has to make it work.

The problem is not always the result of experts working in isolation. Quite often the staff expert seeks the help of the manager but is told that the manager is too busy to work with him. This is partly due to the lack of an adequate reward system, as discussed above. Work on task forces and teams is perceived to be costly and time consuming, and usually this perception is true. However, at this point lateral relations must be viewed in perspective, as being just one design strategy of four possible alternatives. The theory being put forth here is that *as organizations introduce new products, new processes, or a diversified product line, the organization must incur greater costs. It has no choice. The choice relates only to the form in which the cost is incurred.* It can be incurred in the form of extended schedules (slack), reduced specialization (self-containment), more computer time and clerical effort (vertical information system), or time and effort from line managers (lateral relations). Thus participation on a task force or team is a cost but it is a natural consequence of the total task being performed by the organization. Alternatives to lateral relations may be more costly.

In order to assure the cooperation of line managers in task forces, the organization must be designed so that the cost of lateral relations is reflected in the budgets of the managers, so that they can legitimately be expected to provide staff for task forces and teams. It will mean that they are more likely to send competent personnel rather than merely someone they can spare. It also communicates to the manager that the organization as a whole thinks that teams are an important part of the decision process. These changes to the budget and reward system have substantial effects on the organization norms which support group decision processes.

The participation of line managers is essential if task forces or teams are to reduce information overloads. This means the group must arrive at an action decision. Therefore the manager who is responsible for implementing the action must participate.

3. *Participants Must Have Information Relevant to the Decision.*   If an action decision is to be reached, the participants in the group must have the information relevant to the decisions with which the group is charged. This is another common-sense statement that is frequently violated. All the departments who are significantly affected by a decision should be there. One of the advantages of PERT networks is that they portray the activities to be performed and who is to perform them. This allows easy identification of affected units.

A more subtle aspect of this point is the choice of the level of the organization from which a participant must come. The level will vary with each department, depending on the pattern of interdependence and task uncertainty within each department. For example, a frequent violator of the appropriate level is the technical function of an organization. The technical representative sometimes comes from too high in the organization. Then during a problem solving session, the representative is too far removed from the technology to be able to evaluate consequences of others' suggestions or to create technical alternatives to satisfy the criteria of other departments. One response to the lack of detailed knowledge is to bring subordinates in with the manager. This has the defect of enlarging the size of the group solving the problem. In one company, such a meeting brought out 40 people. The appropriate solution is to have lower-level personnel represent the department. These people are usually first- and second-level technical people. They are the ones who are in day-to-day contact with the technology.

4. *Participants Must Have the Authority to Commit Their Department.*

If an action decision is to be reached, the participants must be able to commit the resources necessary to carry out the agreed-upon solution. A typical violator of this requirement is the production or operating department. In one company a task force was formed to help manage the introduction of a new product. After one intense confrontation concerning a schedule slippage, the group decided that the best response was for manufacturing to work 100 hours of overtime. The manufacturing representative then stated that he could not commit his organization for that magnitude of resource usage. When the solution was presented to his superior for consideration, it was vetoed. This had a disastrous effect on the group. It achieved effectiveness only when the superior became the representative from manufacturing.

All the above factors are necessary if the task forces and teams are to reach effective action decisions. If any of these factors are missing, the task force may still be useful for other purposes, such as recommendations, fact finding, information sharing, etc. But if information overloads are to be relieved by lateral relations, the group must arrive at and carry out decisions that would normally have been made at higher levels. This means that line managers must participate, be willing to participate, and come from that level of the organization which has both the relevant information and the authority to commit resources. The result will be a high-quality decision and the necessary commitment to implement it. If any of these factors are missing, the team will become one more case of "we tried it and it didn't work."

5. *Influence Based on Knowledge and Information.* One of the consequences of having representatives with authority and relevant information is that the team may be composed of people from different levels of the organization. This will occur if there are differences in subtask uncertainty and interdependence. Recall that structural variations between organizations also exist between departments within organizations. The predictable, interdependent tasks of the operating department lead to concentration of information and authority at high levels. The uncertain diverse tasks of the technical function concentrate authority and information at low levels. Therefore the task forces should represent diagonal cuts across the organization. In order to be effective the status differences must be dealt with so as not to constrain the problem solving process. This requires a norm in the organization that influence is based on knowledge and information rather than on hierarchical position.

In organizations with stable, repetitive tasks and a reasonably effective managerial selection process, there is not likely to be a conflict between hierarchical influence and knowledge-based influence. But in organizations characterized by change and high technology, a single manager cannot know enough about all decision factors. The influence structure for one decision is not the best for another decision. The best influence distribution varies with the decision in question. The organization has to have norms which support knowledge-based influence. If the organization is going to use diagonal-cut teams and does not have the supporting norms, then the organization development effort should be aimed at a culture change to create these norms.[7] If status barriers remain, then the groups will not be effective units for solving problems and making decisions.[8]

6. *The Lateral Processes Must Be Integrated into the Vertical Processes.*
The team decision processes are not intended to undermine but to complement the normal budgeting and resource allocation decisions. Lateral processes are used in addition to vertical processes. They are not replacements. The lateral processes are necessitated by the need for more decision making at low levels. Therefore these processes need to be integrated into the normal day-to-day decision processes.

Nothing irritates a manager more than to have information about his responsibilities "go around" him. The company represented in Figure

8 had this problem. The wing team met and discovered a quality problem. The solution to the problem required some substantial schedule changes which were made by the production control representative. Later in the day, the plant manager held his normal staff meeting. At the meeting, the production control manager was asked by the plant manager how the changes were proceeding. This was the first time he had heard of the changes. The manager's reaction was to limit the discretion of the team representatives. Since a limit to the discretion of team members would limit the decision effectiveness of the teams, the change was not carried out. Instead a procedure was instituted whereby team representatives came in each morning of a meeting, checked the information relevant to their function and team, checked with their superiors if necessary, and then went to the team meeting. Following the team meeting, each unit holds its own meeting to review team actions and unresolved problems. The unresolved problems then become part of the agenda for the plant manager's meeting in the afternoon. The result is a global information system for the plant decision process.

This is also a good example of a system-wide organization development effort. The production control manager could not have achieved the final solution by himself. The integration of team decision processes into existing decision processes requires system-wide intervention. Lack of integration, by generating several actions like the production control manager's initial solution, will create the claim, "We tried it and it didn't work!"

7. *Part-Time, Full-Time Composition.*   When a task force is formed which will operate for a substantial period of time (more than a couple of months), there is a choice of assignment methods. A man can be totally relieved of departmental duties and assigned full time to the task force. Alternatively, he can be partially relieved and work part time for the department and part time on the task force. This is a constant decision in project-oriented organizations. Even though the organization may be functional or matrix, employees may work on several projects at a time or on only one at a time. Marquis reports some data, shown in Table I, which bear on this question.[9]

The study concerns ratings of overall technical, cost, and schedule performance for 37 projects performed for DOD and NASA. The data suggest that a small core of full-time people and a majority of part-time participants will lead to superior performance.

If everyone in a project is working on it full time, all the participants are motivated to identify with a complete piece of work and with the group of people performing it. This advantage is offset by a loss of contact with people within the same department or in this case same technical specialty. There is a greater lack of contact with one's specialty if all people on the project are physically located together. This frequently happens around a project. The result is that scientists are cut off from the pooled resources of their specialty departments. Since most technical information is transmitted verbally through personal interactions, these scientists are cut off from information sources which can provide problem solutions.[10]

Table I

Composition	Number of projects	Project performance[*]
All full time	12	4.6
Over 50% full time	6	3.8
Under 50% full time	13	2.2
All part time	6	3.9

[*]The lower the rating the better the performance.

The other extreme, a project with all part-time participants, maximizes contacts with colleagues but loses the motivational and integrative advantages of identification with a project. A mixture of full-time and part-time personnel provides the best of both worlds. However, there is a substantial difference between the over 50% and under 50% full-time staff. Although this is admittedly post hoc reasoning, little is gained from a motivational and cooperative standpoint by expanding the full-time core. If we have a project employing 50 people, a full-time core of 5 to 10 seems sufficient. If expanded to 25 or 30 full-time people located together, little is gained motivationally. The larger the size of the group, the more likely is it that subgroups will form, and the less each individual participates in overall group decisions. Thus it seems that motivational effects are subject to diminishing returns and information sources are cut off as each additional individual becomes full time. In addition, from an overall organizational point of view, higher proportions of part-time participants permit greater manpower flexibility.[11] This allows the use of more specialized personnel without the expense of partial utilization of their time. This flexibility is one of the primary advantages of matrix-type organizational designs (see Chapter 7).

Some qualifications are in order. The cost of being cut off from colleagues in a technical specialty is a function of the rapidity of change of the knowledge base underlying the specialty. By this reasoning, the cost of separation is small for an accountant but large for a plasma physicist. Thus full-time task force assignments may be preferrable for purely administrative questions.

8. *Conflict Resolution Practices.*   All the previous points dealt with factors which are contextual or antecedent to the actual group decision process. The intent was to remove as many barriers as possible which might constrain the individual from choosing behaviors that are most conducive to effective group problem solving. The reason these factors were treated at some length is that there will be conflict, sometimes considerable conflict, to be resolved when the group convenes. That is, the decision alternative that is most preferred by one department's criteria may be the least preferred by another department's. However, it is assumed that the conflict is good. It is assumed that individuals when faced with conflict will share information about their preferences, about why they have these preferences, and then search out new alternatives which satisfy the criteria of as many departments as possible. The result will be a high quality decision from the point of view of the overall organization.

In order for people to behave as described above, in the face of conflict, they must invest a great deal of emotional and intellectual energy. The appropriate changes suggested in the previous seven discussions all increase the probability that the individual will be willing to incur these psychological costs.

In addition to the problem solving or confrontation mode, there are other resolution practices which can be used. However, they are predicted to be less effective.[12] One approach is for individuals to push for acceptance of the alternative which is preferred by their department and occassionally "give in" by making incremental changes to it, i.e., a bargaining or compromise approach. It is less effective because the conflict does not trigger a search for new alternatives. In addition, the likelihood of getting the department's preferred alternative accepted is increased if information is withheld rather than shared. Under this mode, individuals are less likely to search for better solutions and are less likely to find one if they do search.

A bargaining approach develops when solving the problem is less important than gaining an advantage over the other persons. This occurs when there is competition among the departments from which the participants come. Then each participant represents a constituency. His rewards depend on how closely the solution resembles the departmentally preferred alternative, not on solving the problem in the best interest of the organization. Therefore, reward systems and resource allocation practices should not stimulate competition among interdependent departments.

Another strategy is the prevention of conflict or smoothing over of differences. This sometimes results from bad experiences with the bargaining approach. It can also result from a culture where politeness is valued or from individuals who do not want to bear the emotional costs of confrontation. In these cases, conflict is regarded as bad. The approach is less effective because it eliminates the search which is triggered by conflict. Besides, the conflict is still present but driven underground and acted out in ways which may not contribute to organizational goals.

The last approach is called forcing. It consists of the power of position or knowledge being used to force a preferred alternative on the rest of the group. Although forcing is not generally recommended, it can result in effective decision making. This will be true if the forced alternative is consistent with organizational goals and the act of forcing does not limit future confrontation and information sharing. Forcing will lead to ineffective decisions if it is the dominant mode. If one function or dominant department always forces, then there is no need for a group effort, since information from other departments is ignored. Suboptimal decisions and poor implementation result when a forced solution is based on local information in the presence of interdependence.

The preferred approach to conflict resolution therefore is to use confrontation and problem solving backed up by occasional forcing when lack of agreement stymies the group.[13] Indeed there may be occasional instances when bargaining and smoothing are necessary. Occasionally situations arise which approximate a fixed resource pool, and this triggers bargaining. Similarly smoothing might be used to allow someone to preserve his self-respect so that he can confront and solve problems in the future. But the predominant mode must be confrontation.[14]

9. *Group and Interpersonal Skills.*   The successful use of confrontation in conflict resolution requires that participants have skills to deal with the interpersonal and group decision issues which arise. All factors in the situation, the feelings of the participants as well as so-called "objective facts," should be considered. The conflict resolution process causes individuals to be confronted, to place their egos on the line, to accept criticism, and to deal with role conflict due to multiple group memberships. In order to deal with these feelings, interpersonal competence is essential. It results either from selection or from training. Therefore, organization development activities are required to support the team decision process. Team building activities reduce threat and create a climate in which confrontation can be accepted.

10. *Leadership.*   The occasional use of forcing from a leadership position raises the question of who should be the leader of the team or task force. The problem solving approach is intended to achieve a consensus which obviates the need for a powerful leader. Consensus is not unanimity but a state of affairs in which the individual who disagrees with the preferred solution feels as follows:

> I understand what most of you would like to do. I personally would not do that, but I feel that you understand what my alternative would be. I have had sufficient opportunity to sway you to my point of view but clearly have not been able to do so. Therefore, I will go along with what most of you wish to do.[15]

However, this state of affairs is not always achieved. Sometimes a forced solution is required to achieve some collective action. Then from whose point of view does the decision get forced?

There are several models. One is that a decision is forced from the point of view of an obviously high-status, dominant department. This may be the physicians in hospitals or scientists in aerospace. The group process gives other departments their "day in court," but the burden is on them to convince the high-status department. This process can be effective if the goals of the organization are congruent with those of the high-status department. When they are not, the high-status department adjusts on the basis of information provided by other departments.

Another model occurs when the decision in question predominantly affects one department more than the others. Then the manager of that department becomes the team leader. If consensus is not reached and the leader forces a decision on the others, the organization is still likely to achieve a high-quality decision. The leader must make it clear, however, that it is lack of concensus that causes forcing. Otherwise problem solving may be discouraged in future meetings. He still needs information from interdependent departments.

A variation of this model arises when the predominantly affected department varies with time. For example, in the early stages of introducing a new product, the decisions are primarily technical. A little later they have impact primarily on the production department. At the end, major decisions bear on marketing strategy. The leadership function will pass from one department manager to the next as the questions vary. At each stage, if a decision is forced, it is forced from the point of view of the predominantly affected department but after other departments have had a chance to influence the decision. There is a high probability that these decisions will be in the best interest of the organization.

These models are not sufficient, as more decisions and more decisions of consequence are made and carried out at low levels in the organization. As uncertainty increases, greater care should be taken for the quality of decisions reached through group processes. Other factors change also. There may not be an obviously dominant function. It is often important to get marketing opinion on new products at an early stage. Departments with exclusive access to information may inordinately dominate decision making. When these pressures occur in the presence of increasing differentiation between departments, a need arises for an integration function to bring a global viewpoint into the decision process. In addition someone may work full time on maintaining the quality of the decisions. This role is that of the integrator, the topic for Chapter 7.

SUMMARY

This chapter has introduced the concept of lateral relations and their design. Direct contact, liaison roles, task forces, and teams have been discussed. They were identified as mechanisms by which the organization can move decisions down into the organization toward the points where information originates. This process reduces the information overload by moving decisions to lower levels, freeing higher levels for only consequential and long range decisions. In order to bring global information to bear on the decisions, the organization has to engage in joint decisions. From an information processing point of view, lateral relations reduce overload. But they only work if people behave in a confronting, problem solving manner.

Most of the chapter was concerned with the climate, both representational and procedural, which must support the joint decision process. The joint decision process must include line managers from the level of the organization which has both the information relevant to the decision and the authority to commit resources to implement the decision. The processes of assigning people to groups, rewarding performance, and budgeting resources must support the group processes. These formal organization practices "communicate" to individuals how important these groups are and influence their willingness to incur the psychological costs of confrontation. The group processes must also be integrated into the organization's decision process. The climate may be supportive, but participants must also have the skills to deal with interpersonal issues which necessarily arise. Finally the leadership should come from the department whose viewpoint is most congruent with organizational goals relevant to the decision. If this department cannot be found and decisions reached by groups are consequential, it pays to design the role of integrator to perform the leadership function.

All these factors can facilitate the joint decision process. The organization development effort of the organization must diagnose which factors need to be changed and intervene to make them support the joint decision process.

NOTES

0. Melville Dalton, *Men Who Manage* (New York: John Wiley, 1957).
1. George F. Farris, "Organizing Your Informal Organization," *Innovation,* October 1971.
2. Alvin Zander and Donald Wolfe, "Administrative Rewards and Coordination among Committee Members," *Administrative Science Quarterly,* June 1964, pp. 50–69.
3. William M. Newport, "The Interdepartmental Transfer: An Integrative Strategy," (Cambridge, Mass.: M.I.T., 1969), unpublished M.S. thesis.
4. M. Kanno, "Effects on Communication Between Labs and Plants of the

Transfer of R & D Personnel" (Cambridge, Mass.: M.I.T., 1968), unpublished M.S. thesis.

5. Harry Weiner, "Role Perception and Organization Ineffectiveness in the Foreign Service" (Cambridge, Mass.: M.I.T., 1970), unpublished M.S. thesis.

6. Edgar Schein, "The Reluctant Professor: Implications for University Management," *Sloan Management Review,* Fall 1970, pp. 35–50.

7. See Richard Beckhard, *Organization Development: Strategies and Models* (Reading, Mass.: Addison-Wesley, 1969), Chapter 4.

8. Edwin M. Bridges, Wayne J. Doyle, and David J. Mahan, "Effects of Hierarchical Differentiation on Group Productivity, Efficiency, and Risk Taking," *Administrative Science Quarterly,* September 1968, pp. 305–319.

9. Donald Marquis, "Ways of Organizing Projects," *Innovation,* No. 5, 1969, pp. 26–33.

10. Thomas J. Allen and Stephen Cohen, "Information Flow in Research and Development Laboratories," *Administrative Science Quarterly,* March 1969, pp. 12–20.

11. Richard A. Goodman, "Organization and Manpower Utilization in Research and Development," *IEEE Transactions,* December 1968, pp. 198–204.

12. Robert R. Blake and Jane S. Mouton. *The Managerial Grid* (Houston, Texas: Gulf Publishing Co., 1964).

13. Paul Lawrence and Jay Lorsch, *Organization and Environment* (Boston: Harvard Business School, 1967), pp. 73–78.

14. The management of conflict is treated in depth elsewhere in this series; see Richard Walton, *Interpersonal Peacemaking: Confrontations and Third Party Consultation* (Reading, Mass.: Addison-Wesley, 1969).

15. Edgar Schein, *Process Consultation: Its Role in Organization Development* (Reading, Mass.: Addison-Wesley, 1969), p. 56.

Chapter 6
A CASE STUDY—TEAMS

The concepts of the previous chapter can be illustrated by a case example. This chapter first presents the organization structure, technology, and current state of affairs facing a manufacturing company. Then we consider the various design strategies that are alternatives to relieve the current situation. Finally we discuss the alternative that was actually chosen.

SITUATION BEFORE THE CHANGE

The manufacturing company in question produces a number of different assembled mechanical devices for the aircraft industry. Many of the devices are used to actuate the flaps, ailerons, stabilizers, and other moving parts of the airframe. About 75 percent of the production goes to airframe manufacturers, while the other 25 percent goes to the airlines as replacement parts. The company has been working with the airframe manufacturers for many years and is quite profitable.

Organization

The 1100 employees are organized in a basic functional structure which is depicted in Figure 9. The department of administration handles the accounting and personnel functions. The process engineering function is

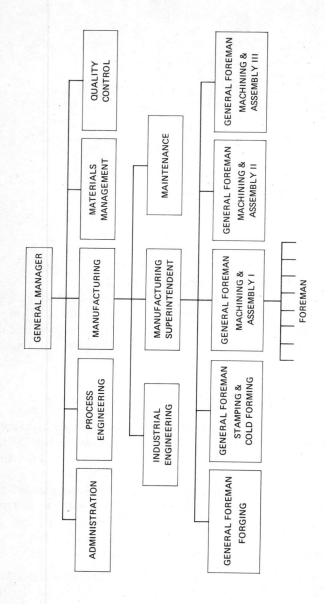

Fig. 9 Organization chart for the manufacturing company.

responsible for the development and design of manufacturing processes and tools. In addition, they manage the construction, maintenance, and set-ups of all tooling. This function is very important since between 20 and 30 percent of the products change each year. Each change requires a retooling effort.

The materials management unit is responsible for scheduling the workflow from vendors to customers. The receiving, shipping, parts control, and purchasing departments make up the remainder of the materials function. They also coordinate with the corporate marketing function. The quality control unit is responsible for inspection of material when it arrives, at intermittent points, and prior to shipping. The high quality standards of the aircraft manufacturers have made this unit an important one.

The majority of the people work in manufacturing. Each of the general foreman has from 9 to 14 foremen working with him. The foremen averaged about 16 in each of their groups. The industrial engineers were concerned with work methods, time standards for costs and schedules, and plant layout. The maintenance unit was responsible for maintaining all physical facilities other than tooling fixtures.

Workflow

The flow of work from vendors to customers is shown in Figure 10. The flow begins with raw materials in the form of homogeneous, standard steel forms being fed to the forging and stamping operations. These operations convert the standardized pieces into more product-specific forms. The completed parts go to a holding area for in-process inventory. The buffer inventory uncouples the two operating areas. This inventory is partially necessitated by the fact that the efficient batch size for forging is quite different than that for machining and assembly.

There are three machining and assembly operations. Each area produces a range of products which requires the particular machining skills peculiar to the area. These are not product-specialized areas, however. No product has sufficient volume to justify setting up a machining line for that product alone. Therefore the layout has some features of a job shop, in that orders are sequenced through process centers; and it has some features of a flow shop, in that the three areas capitalized on the regularities in the sequence of processes which existed across groups of products.

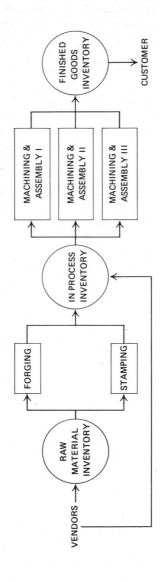

Fig. 10 Work flow at the manufacturing company.

Some of the high volume items were held as finished goods inventory. The inventory was also used for holding replacement parts for which quick delivery was necessary. However, most production was to customer order.

Assessment of Decision Processes

In late 1969 a new general manager assumed office. In the process of learning the business he discovered among the management a dissatisfaction with the prevailing state of affairs. On the surface there was little reason for the dissatisfaction. The profits were at planned levels. The costs were under control. The growth in volume was adequate. But with a little analysis he discovered that managers felt that today's performance was being achieved at the expense of tomorrow's performance.

Most of the top management group felt they were spending almost all their time on day-to-day problems. They were continually being drawn into "now" problems on the shop floor that they felt should be handled at lower levels. The longer-run tooling and capital investment programs were not receiving anywhere near the attention they required. If their programs were not handled well, the neglect would generate more "now" problems next year.

The general manager and the top management team took the analysis of current decision processes as their first order of business. They first analyzed the environment in which they were operating. Everyone was aware of the year-to-year market changes, but they were surprised when the ten-year history was compiled. Although the company still offered the same basic product lines, the individual variations had grown from 400 to 800. The number of parts had gone from 5000 to 8000. The proportion of products requiring retooling every year had jumped from 20 percent to 30 percent. Thus there was a greater variety of products and more frequent changes in the line.

There were some qualitative changes as well. The airframe manufacturers were hard pressed financially. They reduced their inventories but tried to get their vendors to hold the inventory for them or to decrease the delivery time and increase delivery reliability. The quality specifications and tolerance limits continued to get tighter. At the same time the manufacturers and their suppliers had to acquire expertise in working with titanium. This lighter metal was being used extensively on the larger and supersonic aircraft. As with any new technology there were many mistakes and rejected lots.

In the face of these substantial changes, the general manager was surprised that the plant was doing as well as it was. He recognized that the key to success for the plant was efficient scheduling. They had to meet airframe assembly schedules and at the same time fully utilize their capital equipment and high-skilled labor. One response to this state of affairs was to expand by adding multiple shifts. The machines were now running 24 hours a day.

In order to determine how the plant was scheduled, the general manager began an analysis of the production scheduling system in the materials management unit. The materials management group was primarily concerned with aggregate scheduling for the entire plant. They worked from aggregated forecasts and smoothed out the fluctuations in demand to avoid layoffs and overtime. They did this by building up and depleting inventories, using subcontracting for occasional peak periods, and negotiating more favorable delivery schedules with the customer.[1] Their procedures generated a full load for each department, a smooth flow from raw materials to finished goods, and the required coordination between purchasing, production, and marketing.

The materials management department did not assign specific orders to specific machines. They had tried to centralize the detailed scheduling many years before. A number of scheduling boards, mounted on the wall, maintained the availability of each machine group. As orders came in, due dates were negotiated and the order was scheduled in the time available. However, the staff assigned to maintain the boards was very quickly overloaded. In addition to dealing with the arrival of customer orders and cancellations, they had to make changes for machine breakdowns, absenteeism, quality rejects, and engineering changes. After that experience, it was agreed that the materials group would see that the total available time in each shop matched the demand for that shop's services while the detailed job assignment was left to each shop. The materials department assigned due dates for operations, but these served only as guides for production personnel. The due dates were based on historical average lead times and standard times worked out by industrial engineering. As customers requested work by a certain date, the materials function would simply subtract the average lead times from that date and generate start dates which on the average were necessary to complete the order on time. This procedure is referred to as "scheduling for infinite capacity," since capacity constraints are not explicitly considered.[2]

The assessment of the top management team was that this procedure worked well as long as material was available, the aggregate demand equaled the capacity available, and the shop personnel had sufficient flexibility to adapt to short-run schedule conflicts. Since material availability and short-run capacity were not in question, the team's attention shifted to the shop floor.

The scheduling procedure mentioned above had the defect that it created schedule conflicts. In subtracting average lead times from delivery dates, the materials management function did not consider the load already existing on a machine. It was possible to schedule three or four jobs on the same machine at the same time. These conflicts were no problem if the production personnel had some short-run flexibility to shift manpower, selectively schedule overtime, etc. However, analysis by the management team revealed very quickly that the foremen and general foremen did not have the flexibility required. Market changes had increased the number of machine set-ups and tooling changes. Since set-up men and tooling personnel were part of process engineering, the changes increased the dependence of manufacturing upon the engineering service. Also the quality control unit was required to inspect the first few units produced to check the new set-ups and tooling fixtures. While the machine was idle because of the set up and inspection, the foreman would try to get maintenance to perform machine repairs. This coordination was necessary to minimize machine idle time and still meet tight schedules. Thus, there was little flexibility and an increasing amount of interdependence.

In the day-to-day scheduling process, the foremen and general foremen were continually seeking the services of the support units. Quite often two or more demands upon the support unit could not be met simultaneously. Process engineering, quality control, and maintenance were forced into making priority decisions. If there was disagreement, the situations were referred upward to top management. These schedule-related priority issues were the ones that were burdening the top management.

This general problem is present in all organizations when operating units share service and support resources. The problem is one of determining priorities among the requests for service. The normal way to handle the problem is with a schedule. Requests for service are matched against service resources, and priorities are determined at a global level by those knowledgeable about the total situation. Short-run priorities are determined by which job is scheduled first. In the present situation, the number of factors and the rate at which they changed caused the schedule to decay and become useless. Priorities were set through personal contacts. But the head of maintenance could not make priority decisions. He knew his resource availability but not which request for service was more important. Hence the question was escalated to higher levels where priority decisions could be made.

The case description illustrates how external changes are translated into information processing overloads. There were increases in diversity (number of product variations), uncertainty (30 percent tooling changes, titanium technology), required performance levels (tighter schedules, greater delivery reliability, stricter tolerances), and interdependence (engineering-production-maintenance). The increased information processing and decision making overloaded the hierarchy. Therefore some kind of organization design action was required. In the next section the alternative actions are created and described.

ORGANIZATION DESIGN ALTERNATIVES

In order to relieve the overload, the manufacturing firm must choose one or some combination of the four design strategies. Each of the available strategies will be described in this section along with the predicted effects and costs.

Slack

The first strategy that could be adopted would be to employ various forms of slack resources. Three examples will be discussed here. First, the average lead times could be extended. Instead of allowing six weeks from start to finish for an order, the lead time could be extended to eight or nine. The additional time would be effective in removing the overload. The additional time would reduce the necessity of having all support units present simultaneously on a tooling change. Production could tolerate more machine idle time and still meet delivery dates. They could schedule set-ups independent of maintenance work because two work stoppages would not be disruptive. The additional time reduces the interdependence between production and the support units.

The increased lead time has its costs also. On the average there will be two or three weeks' demand in in-process inventory tying up additional working capital. However, the real cost is asking the customer to order eight weeks prior to his planned usage rather than six. The current situation in the industry is one of reducing lead time to four or five weeks rather than six. Thus increasing lead time is very costly. If a finished goods inventory could be accumulated, then production could be uncoupled from the customer's usage. An extended lead time in production and quick delivery to customers would both be possible. However the large variety of products and parts and frequent engineering changes make the carrying of finished goods expensive. In addition, uncertainty about customer specifications means that production is undertaken only when an order is received, rather than in anticipation of demand through inventory accumulation.

A second approach would be to employ additional resources in the form of machines rather than inventory. More machines would have the same effect as longer lead time. They would increase the amount of planned machine idle time. The greater the amount of idle time, the less the need to perform simultaneously all those activities which require the machine to be idle. More machines reduce the interdependence between production and support activities. However, more machinery is expensive. Current technology requires computerized and numerically controlled equipment; it is simply too expensive to leave this equipment under-utilized.

A third approach is to employ more resources in the support units. The first two approaches adapted production operations for the convenience of scheduling support resources. This is letting "the tail wag the dog." With the majority of resources employed in the manufacturing unit, it makes greater economic sense to adapt the operation of the support units. One way is to employ more engineers, inspectors, and maintenance personnel. The more resources in the support units, the fewer the priority problems. The fewer the priority problems, the less the load on the hierarchy. Dalton's analysis of production and maintenance activities reveals that, at budget time, production frequently supports the demands of maintenance for more men in order to remove possible priority problems.[3] However, skilled maintenance specialists and process engineers are also expensive. Whether additional support personnel should be employed depends on the cost of other feasible alternatives.

The costs and effects of employing slack resources should now be clear. Coordination problems arise out of the scarcity of specialized resources. Scheduling and priority problems are eliminated by eliminating the scarcity. The scarcity of specialized resources is eliminated by employing more resources or by eliminating the time pressure. The design problem is to determine which is the scarcest, or bottleneck, resource and what is the least costly way to increase the availability of that resource.

Self-Contained Departments

The second possible design strategy is to create self-contained units. This strategy also reduces the interdependence between production and the support units. The design problems are to select the basis on which the autonomous departments will be created (the departmentalization problem) and the level of the organization to which they will report.

The usual alternative departmental arrangement to the functional design is the product divisional design. However, this is not the case in the present situation. Product divisions are the alternative when coordination problems are caused by new product introductions which pass through functional departments. New products contribute to the scheduling problem in this case but are not its primary cause. Also the costs of equipping each product line with its own machinery would be prohibitive.

Instead of product divisions, the departmental arrangement should place together those roles whose interdependence is causing the priority problem. It is the process engineer, set-up man, quality control inspector, maintenance crew, and production personnel whose activities need to be coordinated in order to simultaneously meet delivery schedules, utilize capital equipment, meet aircraft quality standards, prolong the life of expensive equipment, and utilize skilled labor. If these roles are placed in the same unit, the department will contain all the resources necessary to maintain the schedules. It will be self-contained with respect to meeting due dates set by the materials department. It should be noted that the arrangement will not be self-contained with respect to personnel and industrial relations, new product introductions, accounting information, aggregate scheduling, etc. These decisions will still be coordinated by higher level management.

Once the basis for grouping roles is established, there is the question of organizational level. Should each foreman have a set-up man, engineer, maintenance crew, etc.? This question is constrained by the technology of the workflow. In Figure 10 one can see that the in-process inventory creates two kinds of unit which are independent of each other with respect to detailed scheduling decisions—the forging and stamping units and the three machining and assembly units. In addition, within each unit, the workflows are parallel. There is no sequential interdependence between the two kinds of unit. The workflow and inventory location create five independent units corresponding to areas assigned to the general foremen. Each unit can function independently in the structure, as shown in Figure 11.

The self-contained structure shown in Figure 11 will eliminate the overloads caused by priority decisions on the use of support groups. The problem is solved by dividing up support groups and giving part to each general foreman. The general foreman then resolves the priority issues for his own department, including the assignment of jobs to machines. The general foreman now has the resource flexibility to make the short-run adjustments required in order to schedule to infinite capacity.

The self-contained structure has its costs also. There are a number of cases of fractional use of specialized resources within the self-contained units. In our example, three specialists handle numerically controlled machine tools. However, four of the five units make substantial use of numerically controlled equipment. The firm must either duplicate the specialized resource by hiring another specialist or reduce specialization by employing generalists who handle other equipment in addition to numerically controlled machines. The functional structure pools the fractional uses of specialized resources. But the duplication or lost benefits of specialization may be less costly than the additional slack production resources required by a functional structure.

There are further costs due to lack of career paths for the personnel in the support units. The organization may have difficulty in holding competent engineers and maintenance personnel if promotions to general foreman go to production personnel. In the functional structure there are promotion possibilities within the function. One can remain an engineer and rise to manager of engineering. But the self-contained structure encourages engineers to leave or become generalists. Both options further reduce the benefits of specialization.

In summary, the strategy of creating self-contained units reduces overloads caused by a need for priority decisions; it does so by reducing the amount of sharing of specialized resources. Sometimes reduced sharing is accompanied by a reduced number of specialized roles. The design problem is to decide which roles are to be combined into a self-contained unit and to what level of organization the combination will report.

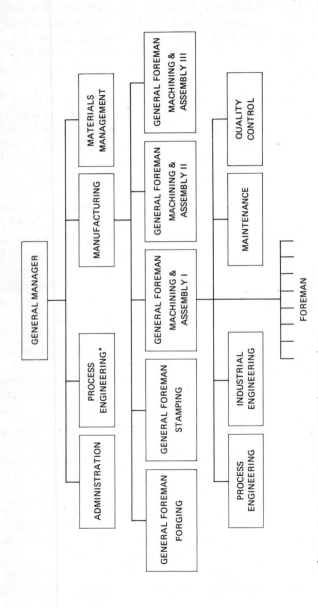

*Responsible for developing new processes for new products.

Fig. 11 Self-contained structure.

Vertical Information System

The third design strategy available to the organization is to employ the new information technology in the detailed scheduling process. Unlike the two previous strategies, implementing the new information technology seeks to adapt the organization's decision processes to the new task requirements. The demand characteristics, technology, lead times, and division of labor are accepted as given.

The strategy requires the creation of a current, global data base and a decision mechanism capable of manipulating the data so as to reach decisions concerning the scheduling of all resources. In our example, resource availability information is currently scattered. Each unit has the information only about its own resources. It employs a local–real time structure. It is possible, however, to construct a computer program and file structure to record the status of all machines, maintenance crews, set-up men, engineers, and quality control inspectors and to schedule their utilization.

The key to the effectiveness of this strategy is to keep the schedule current in the face of a multitude of changes. The earlier attempt at centralized scheduling was overwhelmed, and it only attempted to schedule machines. A real-time system with remote terminals in all departments can keep a current status record on the availability of all resources. In addition, it can record changes in customer orders, quality rejects, and engineering changes, and it can adapt schedules to erroneous time estimates for production jobs, set-ups, and machine repair. The maintenance of a current data base and schedule requires a great deal of computer time, input-output units, and supporting personnel. However it will remove the overload problem. While the author is aware of no operating systems for this strategy, there is a comparable research project concerned with scheduling aircraft maintenance.[4]

The effects and costs of this strategy are straightforward. The priority decisions concerning the use of specialized resources are made by bringing together in a single place, probably the materials management function, all information about resource availability and resource demands. The global information is gathered from the shop floor, maintenance crews, engineers, and inspectors via terminals scattered throughout the plant. The information is manipulated and a schedule produced by a man-machine problem solving combine. The result is efficient scheduling and a management structure relieved of day-to-day decisions. All this is gained by means of a substantial investment in computer hardware, peripheral equipment, programming effort, and computer time.

Lateral Relations

The fourth design alternative is to employ and formalize decision processes which cross lines of authority. The purpose is to move priority decisions down to lower levels of the organization. The design issues revolve around who should be represented, what the mechanism should be, and at what organization level the mechanism should operate.

The current organization uses lateral relationships of the informal type. Indeed these personal contacts and upward referral resulting from their overload are the chief manifestation of the current problem. When there were fewer set-ups and tooling changes, easier schedule deadlines, and fewer products, the informal direct contacts and task forces were adequate to secure coordination. But currently these processes are not adequate. When two or three people get together they never seem to have all the information needed to make a decision. Attempts to gather all informed parties is all but impossible. It is easier to refer the problem up to the next level. Thus the informal, spontaneous personal contacts which worked well in the past need to be supplemented. But what form should the supplemental effort take?

The first mechanism on the list is the liaison role. Liaison personnel, particularly in process engineering, would help relieve some of the priority problems. If process engineering would formalize a linking role, that role occupant would perform engineering work and also be responsible for coordinating engineering and manufacturing activities. Similarly, linking roles could be formalized in the other support functions as well. These changes would aid the coordination between manufacturing and engineering and between manufacturing and maintenance, etc. However, liaisons alone are not sufficient. The current problems do not stem from function-to-function links but from multifunction links. Quite often foremen, engineers, maintenance foremen, and inspectors gather together only to find they need schedule information from materials management or standard times from industrial engineering. A mechanism legitimizing multifunction problem solving is required.

The next mechanism would be task forces. Each time a problem arose in manufacturing, the foreman could call together all liaison personnel concerned with his area. The response of the manufacturing manager to this suggestion was that the liaison personnel should be equipped with two-way radios, because such problems arose daily. The manufacturing manager's half-humorous remark led to the proposal of daily meetings of all functional personnel concerned with the work of a manufacturing area. Thus it was suggested that teams were the mechanism for handling multifunctional interdependence at low levels of the organization.

As soon as it was decided that teams were to be the mechanism, new design questions arose. The same factors that are relevant to the departmentalization and level decisions for self-contained structures are relevant for teams. Thus the workflow and inventory locations make the five general foremen the most likely location and level of organization at which the teams should operate. Thus the team model provides the general foreman with a temporary staff rather than the permanent one provided by the self-contained model, but it avoids some of the costs. Once the basis and organizational level are determined, the question arises as to who should go to the team meetings.

The type of functions that should provide representatives was a decision that was quickly resolved in our example. The functions of manufacturing, quality control, process engineering, maintenance, industrial engineering, and materials management were chosen to be permanent members, while accounting and industrial relations would be called on an "as needed" basis. A design problem did arise when the selection of functional representatives was being discussed. If the teams were to arrive at decisions, the participants must have the information relevant to the decisions and the authority to commit their function to the team's choice of alternatives.

All the functions except process engineering could handle the selection very easily. Each of these functions had an authority structure like that shown for maintenance in Figure 12. The organizational units in maintenance were identical to those in manufacturing. To each manufacturing area there corresponded a foreman and maintenance crew to handle most machine repair problems that could arise in that area.

Some specialist skills for which there was not enough work in the individual areas were collected into specialist pools and shared among the areas. In addition there was some maintenance work performed in areas other than manufacturing. The functions of quality control, industrial engineering, and materials management had a similar "mirror im-

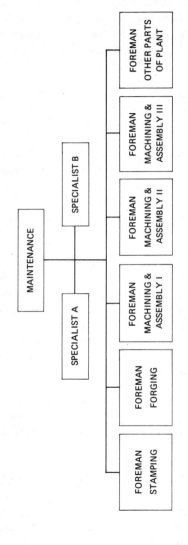

Fig. 12 Functional structure for maintenance which is mirror image of manufacturing.

age plus specialists" type of structure. The maintenance foreman and his counterpart in the other functions were the team members. They had the necessary information and authority.

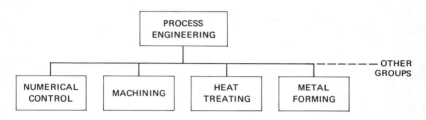

Fig. 13 Before organization chart for process engineering.

The process engineering unit had chosen to divide its work on the basis of common technical problems. A partial organization chart is shown in Figure 13. This structure permitted engineering to maximize the expertise that can be brought to bear on different manufacturing processes. The department was able to keep abreast of the latest technological changes and quickly convert them into tooling and manufacturing processes when these changes were beneficial. This same process knowledge was necessary for the custom design market strategy and for the introduction of new products. Each time a new customer order came in, engineering had to create a way to produce it and still meet price constraints. When a process engineer encountered a problem, the information to solve that problem usually came from his experience or the experience of a colleague who had a similar problem in the past. Unlike research and development, there is no body of literature which deals with unique process problems. The specialist structure facilitated these process design problems by placing together those people with common technical problems.

The company was quite pleased with the performance of the process engineering function. Although the manager of process engineering shared the perception of the top management group on the nature of the shop floor problem, he did not want a solution to that problem to be at the expense of the technical excellence of the process designs. Engineering had to maintain links with the technical community as well as manufacturing. The knowledge base underlying the work of maintenance or quality control was not changing so rapidly. Therefore they could adapt their structures to facilitate coordination with manufacturing without much loss of excellence in their specialty. The manager of process engineering suggested appointing an engineer, with the approval of the general foreman, to each team. However, it was pointed out that if the engineer came from machining, and a problem arose concerning heat treating, the engineer would not have the technical knowledge, the information about resource availability, or the authority to change job assignments if the problem required it. This structure satisfied the requirements for skill specialization but not team coordination. The "mirror image" structure satisfied team coordination requirements but not skill specialization.

After much deliberation, the top management group decided on the structure shown in Figure 14. Five new roles were created for engineering managers which corresponded to the five teams. The other half of the engineering group maintained its current form and would concentrate on new processes, processes for new products, and processes for custom-designed orders. For these tasks specialization is required. All subtasks for which there was less need for specialization, such as set-up men, became part of the five new departments. When there was enough work for full time specialists, they worked for the five new managers. But it was agreed that specialists would be rotated from these units to the new process unit to minimize loss of skill specialization. Thus by splitting engineering into two units, one of liaison and support and one of design, the requirements for specialization and coordination could be met simultaneously. This design was agreed upon and implemented.

The chosen design has its cost also. There are new liaison roles to staff in engineering and perhaps in the other functions. There are costs of disruption in engineering. The positions must be staffed, generalists must be trained, and new training needs and career patterns arise throughout the function. But it is judged that these costs and disruptions are less than those that would be required by the other design alternatives.

It should be pointed out that there are several possible designs which would accomplish the same result. Another organization may not be able to staff the five new roles in engineering immediately and may create an interim design. Still another may create two assistant engineering managers, one in charge of new designs as indicated and one in charge of

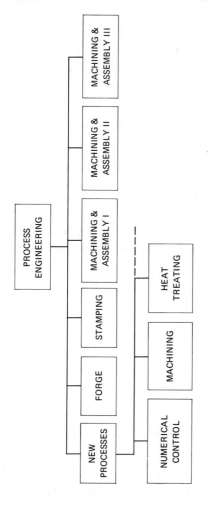

Fig. 14 Differentiated structure for process engineering.

support to which the five new roles would report. These alternatives reflect the fact that the organization may not have the people to staff an ideal structure. The organization must be designed around people as well as task requirements. It is variations such as these that generate the unique features of an organization's structure. The engineering people in the organization are a unique set of individuals, and this fact will be reflected in a unique structure. The alternatives represent variations in degree, not in kind. All of them, in this case, represent some variation on the split between design and support.

We have not attempted to discuss the process used to arrive at the structure. Given the nature of the issues, lower-level engineering personnel should have been involved in order to create an acceptable solution.

In summary, teams were chosen to solve the problem of hierarchical overload, although the other three alternatives would have been feasible. Decisions will be moved to the general foreman level. By creating teams with members who have the information and authority to commit resources, the general foreman will have the necessary flexibility to adapt to changing floor situations. The teams may still encounter problems they cannot solve, but these will be much fewer than before. The implementation of teams will create additional staffing costs for new roles.

TEAMS IN OPERATION

The manufacturing firm actually implemented the team design discussed. At the end of a year's operation, the teams had relieved the previous situation and were operating satisfactorily. Several minor changes were made to the team decision process and probably would continue to be made in the future. The critical adjustment was to make the team processes consistent with the traditional hierarchical processes and with existing personnel.

Early in the implementation, some individuals were having difficulty making the shift from being a member of a function to being a member of a team and back again. When the problem was confronted it was found to originate partially within the functions. Some participants were not fully informed about their function and could not share information they did not have. Others were unsure of the kind of commitments they could make. The problem was not one of having authority or not having authority but one of degree. The attempted solution was to initiate staff meetings within functions prior to the team meetings if this was not done already and to improve those that were held. What was needed was more information and problem sharing within functions so that team participants could be more effective across functions. Reporting back after the team meeting also helped remove the pressures for some participants.

Other individuals still disliked the team role, either because they felt they were being put between two groups or because they disliked generalizing and preferred quality control or engineering problems. Several individuals transferred out of the team roles. It was felt that no one should be penalized for not remaining in the linking position. Thus, through self-selection, individuals who are comfortable with linking roles found their way into the teams.

At the moment several other problems are being addressed. Accounting and materials management are working on new types of information to present to the teams to support their decisions. Industrial relations is examining ways to incorporate specialist team contributions into the performance appraisal and is starting a training program in problem-solving skills. Thus there is always a continual adjustment of team decision making to integrate it into the main organization.

SUMMARY

This chapter has presented a case in order to illustrate the theory being developed here. It was shown how changes in a task may be converted into information processing and hierarchical overloads. Next the framework was used to identify the design alternatives and their costs. In the example, teams were adequate to the task. The general foreman was the obvious leader of the groups. Let us turn to other situations, which require integrating roles to supplement the team processes.

NOTES

1. For an analysis of organizational implications of smoothing problems, see Jay R. Galbraith, "Solving Production Smoothing Problems," *Management Science,* August 1969, pp. B–665 to B–674.
2. For a more complete description, see James C. Emery, "An Approach to Job Shop Scheduling Using a Large Scale Computer," *Industrial Management Review,* Fall 1961, pp. 78–96.
3. Melville Dalton, *Men Who Manage* (New York: John Wiley, 1959), Chapter 3.

4. S. M. Drezner and R. L. Van Horn, "Design Considerations for a Computer-Assisted Maintenance Planning and Control System," Research Memorandum P–3765, The RAND Corporation, February 1968.

Chapter 7

LATERAL RELATIONS: INTEGRATING ROLES AND MATRIX DESIGNS

The use of lateral relations—direct contact, liaison roles, task forces, and teams—permits the organization to make more decisions and process more information without overloading hierarchical communication channels. These channels are reserved for the unique consequential problems which increase in number as uncertainty and diversity of the task increase. Further increases in task uncertainty and diversity result in more decision making at lower levels through joint decision processes.

The increase in the number of decisions and the number of decisions of consequence made at lower levels of the organization increases the dependence of the organization on the quality of the decisions reached through such joint processes. On the one hand, the process itself increases the quality of the decisions. If participants come from the most interdependent departments and from the appropriate level in that department, the potential quality of the decision can be increased. The process involves those individuals who are most knowledgeable about the decision in question. In addition, by involving individuals who are responsible for performing the work, the process increases the motivation to accept and implement the chosen alternative. But since each participant necessarily has only partial information, a high quality decision will result if, and only if, the partial information is shared, built upon, and used to search for and create new alternatives.

To convert a collection of individuals into a problem solving team characterized by openness, trust, and a willingness to confront each other requires interpersonal and group skills and a climate in which group problem solving can take place. Some of the factors determining skills and climate were introduced in Chapter 5. The chapter concluded by suggesting that effective problem solving took place by confrontation backed up by forcing modes of conflict resolution. If this is true, then decision quality depends on the power source from which a forced solution occurs. It was suggested that if a solution is forced from a power base whose goals are consistent with organization goals and in a manner which does not discourage future problem solving, this process can lead to high quality decisions. Further it was suggested that by selecting a leader from the appropriate places in the organization structure, the power source could be controlled and the organization designed to achieve high quality decisions.

This chapter expands on the power bases in the joint decision process.[1] As uncertainty in an organization grows, there is greater dependence on the quality of joint decisions due to the fact that there are more decisions and more decisions of consequence reached through joint decision processes. At moderate levels of uncertainty, a few mistakes are not critical and periodic reviews can correct some of the low quality decisions. This process is not adequate at higher levels of uncertainty and diversity. In addition to the greater number of decisions of consequence, the organization's ability to use confrontation to achieve quality decreases. The reason is that the changes in task uncertainty differentially affect subtasks. Some departments experience large increases in subtask uncertainty, while others experience little or none.

For example, if a firm undertakes a strategy to introduce new products, the technical function experiences a greater increase in subtask uncertainty than the production or accounting function. Two new problems are generated by the increasing differences in subtask uncertainty. (1) Differences in subtask uncertainty create differences in the individual power of participants in joint decisions. Since the organization must take some coordinated action, it requires estimates of future events from functions concerned with uncertain subtasks. Since these estimates can rarely be challenged, those functions with uncertain subtasks have greater power to influence decisions than functions performing routine predictable tasks.[2] The organization design problem is to create a set of conditions such that power differences do not diminish the quality of decisions reached through lateral decisions processes. (2) Differences in subtask uncertainty create differences in the attitudes of the participants in joint decisions. There is some evidence to suggest that the attitudes of decision makers are related to the uncertainty of the tasks they perform.[3] Then as tasks begin to differ in uncertainty, the attitudes of the managers begin to differ also. Another organization design problem is to see that these differences in attitudes, called differentiation, do not reduce the quality of the joint decision process.

Thus the organization design question is, what factors can the organization change so as to create a distribution of power and influence that will result in high quality decisions? Very briefly the organization (1) creates a new role and (2) designs enough power and influence into it to bring about high quality joint decisions. Before describing the role, however, we need to explain the concept of differentiation and relate it to the framework being developed throughout the book.

DIFFERENTIATION

Differentiation as defined by Lawrence and Lorsch is ". . . the difference in cognitive and emotional orientation among managers in different functional departments." The concept suggests that the attitudes of managers become differentiated in several dimensions to the degree that the tasks they manage differ in uncertainty and time span of feedback.[5] In Chapter 6, one of the dimensions of differentiation (not necessarily related to uncertainty), goal orientation, was discussed. The fact that different departments preferred different alternatives as a solution to the same problem was the basic source of conflict. Now as subtasks increase in uncertainty, differences in other dimensions also become large enough to be causes of conflict.

First, departments vary in the formality of their structures. The highly predictable tasks in operations lead to explicit measures of performance, well-defined procedures, narrow spans of control, and well-defined areas of authority and responsibility. In contrast the technical function, with its uncertain task, does not have the clearly defined procedures, responsibilities, and performance measures. It does not because it cannot, given the nature of its task.

Second, individuals in these departments vary in their orientation toward time. The technologist spends hours analyzing ambiguous problems and uncertain relationships in order to complete a design due in three months. He will not know if it is successful until a moon shot is completed two years from now. Contrast him with the operations foreman, who quickly loads three jobs on his machines, shifts manpower assignments, ships two completed lots, and knows at the end of the day how well he has performed. These different time perspectives are necessary for their respective tasks.

Finally each department develops languages of its own. As groups of people continuously share a common set of problems, they develop shorthand ways of referring to activities and events. Technical departments hire people who have been trained and know the language of the department's specialty. Such a language permits people to communicate more efficiently by transmitting more information with fewer symbols. However, despite the fact that specialized languages increase efficiency of communication within a department, they decrease efficiency between departments.

There may be other dimensions, e.g., risk-taking propensity, which may be relevant in specific situations, but the dimensions we have already described are general enough to illustrate the concept of differentiation. In addition each dimension has the following attributes.

1. A relationship between the dimension and task uncertainty is necessary for effective subtask performance.[6] The better the fit between the subtask, the formality of structure, the orientation toward time, and the language, the more effective is subtask performance.

2. While differentiation is associated with effective subtask performance, it is also associated with difficulty in establishing collaboration between differentiated departments.[7] It makes it more difficult to employ lateral relations to coordinate interdependent tasks. It makes a consensus more difficult to obtain.

The problem facing the differentiated organization is how to obtain overall task integration among departments *without reducing the differences that lead to effective subtask performance.* The relationships between engineering and production can be made more cooperative by having engineering work on day-to-day quality problems, take a short-run orientation, and use cost rather than technical elegance as the choice criterion. While this will improve cooperation, it will not create new technology for tomorrow's products. Similarly, conflicts should not be resolved by changing goal orientations (although sometimes an operational global goal can be found), but by searching for new alternatives which satisfy differentiated subgoals of the interdependent departments.

Thus as organizations adopt strategies which result in more task uncertainty, the departments performing subtasks become more differentiated since subtasks vary in task uncertainty, language, and goals. So at the very time that the organization needs more effective interdepartmental decision making, cooperation becomes more difficult.

INTEGRATING ROLE

The response of the organization to the concern for decision quality is to create new roles in the organization structure. These roles are called integrating roles.[8] The managers who occupy them do not supervise any of the actual work. Instead they assist those who do, so that the work is coordinated in the best interests of the organization. This is the general manager's job, but he does not have the time when the organization's tasks become diverse and uncertain. The integrator becomes a little general manager with responsibility for a particular decision process.

Integrating roles are a general phenomenon, but the labels vary in particular situations. In manufacturing firms with significant logistics problems, the integrator is a "materials manager." If the functional departments involved in the workflow (such as purchasing, manufacturing, traffic, and physical distribution) each minimized its own costs, they would not achieve an overall optimum for the entire logistics system. The task of the materials manager is to coordinate all the scheduling and inventory decisions so that they are made in the best interests of the firm. For business firms with diverse product lines that change rapidly, the integrator is a "product manager." He coordinates decisions made in each function that relate to his product or product line. In aerospace firms and government agencies, the integrator is a "project manager" or "program manager." In hospitals the "unit manager" coordinates and integrates the decisions of doctors, nurses, dieticians, and service personnel for a particular ward or building.

In each case, the task of the integrator is not to do the work but to coordinate the decision process. In each case, his decisions concern matters that are consequential for the organization and that are diverse and uncertain enough to overload the general manager. Rather than change the authority structure to contain the decision process, the integrator role is created to coordinate the process across the interdependent departments. The difficulty is that the integrator needs to be able to influence the decision making behavior of individuals who do not work for him. The organization design question becomes one of how much and what kind of power and authority should be designed into the integrating role.

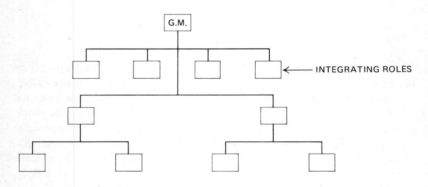

Fig. 15 Integrating roles representing little general managers.

As this role first evolves, it usually reports to the general manager, as indicated in Figure 15. The integrators have no formal authority and no staff working for them. It is their function to bring the general manager perspective to bear on joint decision problems arising at various levels of the organization which concern their decision area. They do this by acting as chairman of task forces and teams considering joint problems, by pulling information together in one place, and by giving full-time attention to problems arising from uncertainty. The question remains, however, how does the integrator exercise influence if he has no formal authority?

The Integrator Has Contacts.   The integrating role has a wide range of contacts and exposures. The most significant contact is the general manager. The integrator, by his reporting relationship, has the ear of the most powerful individual in the organization. A mention of the fact that Paul Jones from engineering is doing a superb job on the product team can give Paul Jones, four levels down, an exposure he would not otherwise have. Similarly he can influence the reward system by passing on the same information to the engineering manager. This provides an unsolicited, outside evaluation which has to be considered.

The integrator should have wide contacts across departments also. For example, Paul Jones mentions that he has a new idea but his boss is not helping him push it. The integrator, however, takes it to marketing and finds a sales manager who has a customer with a similar need. The result is that Paul Jones has a project of his own. The example could be multiplied many times. The point is that the integrator is at the crossroads of several information streams. What might appear as an interesting but worthless fact to a marketing manager may be a valuable piece of information to the technical function. By identifying these situations and following through with them the integrator performs useful functions for the departments. He becomes a useful rather than a "pushy" guy. He exercises influence based on access to information. The influence is in the direction of meeting both individual and organizational goals.

The Integrator Establishes Trust.   The integrator equalizes power differences and increases trust in the joint decision processes. The need for power equalization and trust arises because of the differential effect of task uncertainty. Some subtasks become more uncertain than others. The departments managing these uncertain subtasks acquire power due to the process of uncertainty absorption.

> Uncertainty absorption takes place when inferences are drawn from a body of evidence and the inferences, instead of the evidence itself, are then communicated.[10]

As subtasks increase in uncertainty, the amount of uncertainty absorbed increases, because information enters organizations at specific points, and recipients of communications often have neither the time nor knowledge to judge the validity of a communication. Since they rarely can check the validity of a communicated fact, the participants in a joint decision depend on the uncertainty-absorbing department to draw inferences in an objective and valid manner. Thus the greater the subtask uncertainty, the greater is the dependence upon and therefore power of the uncertainty-absorbing department.

The quality of joint decisions is a direct function of how this power is exercised and how the dependent participants perceive the exercise of power. Since the participants cannot examine the evidence directly, their perception of the inferences rests squarely on their confidence and trust in the uncertainty-absorbing department and their knowledge of its biases. If they perceive that the inferences are consistently drawn in a manner to benefit the department rather than the organization, they will counter the department with coalitions, and the joint decision process will degenerate into bargaining. Then the best self-interest strategies are information concealment and distortion. The search for alternatives is deprived of the information needed for high quality decisions. Therefore, when uncertainty absorption takes place, the quality of the joint decisions is highly dependent on the confidence and trust among the participants.

The necessary confidence and trust are difficult to maintain in the context of high differentiation. The production superintendent finds it difficult to have confidence in a bearded, tieless scientist who does not arrive at the office until 9:30, is five minutes late to meetings, and who does not know who won Sunday's football game. However, it is possible to establish trust in this context without reducing the essential attitudinal differences by the proper staffing and use of the integrator role.

The integrating role is ideally staffed when the occupant has demonstrated competence in the areas of greatest uncertainty absorption and has an orientation towards organizational goals rather than parochial goals. Then when an inference is communicated as a fact in the presence of the integrator, there is greater confidence among the recipients in the source of the communique. The reason is that the mere presence of the integrator eliminates the possible distortion of inferences to the parochial interest of the uncertainty-absorbing department. For example, during a problem solving session, a manufacturing manager might suggest that if the product could be redesigned in a particular way, his problems would be easier. The engineering participant might suggest that the change cannot be made because of some law of aerodynamics. The manufacturing manager, since he knows nothing about aerodynamics and therefore has no way of validating the engineer's response, may doubt the engineer. He may challenge the engineer, believing that engineers never accept ideas that they did not create themselves. The problem for the engineer becomes one of defending himself rather than solving the problem. If, however, an integrator is present who knows the laws of aerodynamics and who is part of the general manager's office rather than a member of engineering, the manufacturing manager is more likely to believe the engineer. The presence of an integrator eliminates the possibility that someone with access to knowledge and information can use it as a power source in bargaining.

The integrator equalizes power and increases trust, however, only if he is knowledgeable in the uncertainty-absorbing areas and unbiased with respect to the participating departments. If he is biased, the integrator has the same trust problem as the uncertainty-absorbing department. If he is not knowledgeable, the participants will trust him but he is no more able than they to detect a power abuse. Thus the role occupant needs to be both unbiased and knowledgeable, for his influence rests upon those attributes. With a high level of trust and confidence among the participants to a joint decision, there is greater likelihood of a confrontation mode of conflict resolution and therefore of high quality decisions.

The Integrator Manages Decision Making.   The integrator also exercises influence by managing the joint decision process, rather than making the decision himself. He should perform the integrative or leadership function that is necessary in reaching high quality joint decisions.[11] It was mentioned earlier that merely bringing people together who possess the necessary information to solve a problem does not guarantee that they will use it. The problem solving process needs to be managed. Some attributes of joint decision participants may be either an asset or a liability, depending on how the process is managed. For example, differences of opinion can lead either to hard feelings and bargaining or to confrontation and problem solving. Whether they are an asset or a liability depends critically upon the performance of the discussion leadership function. This requires a role that is different from the roles of the other participants in the joint decision.

> For a leader, such functions as rejecting or promoting ideas according to his personal needs are out of bounds. He must be receptive to information contributed, accept contributions without evaluating them (posting contributions on a chalk board to keep them alive), summarize information to facilitate integration, stimulate exploratory behavior, create awareness of problems of one member by others, and detect when the group is ready to resolve differences and agree to a unified solution.[12]

The integrator's role is not to make the best decision but to see that the best decision gets made.

In order to perform this role the integrator needs to be knowledgeable about the areas in question, capable of crossing attitudinal barriers and seeing things from different points of view, and able to speak the languages of the different specialties which are party to the decision. This multilingual ability is needed so that summaries and restatements can be used to prevent misunderstandings. He must be able to listen to a proposal in "marketing talk" and restate it in "engineering talk." Thus the use of integrators achieves coordination without eliminating the differences—languages, attitudes, etc.—that promote good subtask performance.

The integrator with no formal authority, therefore, does have a power base from which he can influence the decision process for which he is responsible. It is expert power based on knowledge and access to information. The integrator will be effective only if his influence facilitates the coordination of those individuals who have the formal authority and if his power is not seen as contrary to or as a replacement for the formal authority of the participants in the joint decision. The integrator should conceive of his role as a facilitating one rather than a doing one. He is not to do the work but to see that the work that is done is performed in a manner which gives integrity to his product, program, unit, etc.

By its staffing decision, the organization controls the amount of power exercised by the integrator. He has power only if he has the knowledge and behavioral skills to act as an information collector, summarizer, and group discussion leader. Some of the attributes required by the role occupant are obvious from the preceding discussion. He must have knowledge of all the specialties to be integrated and especially of the specialty absorbing the most uncertainty. He must also be unbiased; this factor can be controlled by the reward system for the integrator and by the level to which he reports in the hierarchy, as well as by the original selection of the individual. But he also requires a personality which permits him to use expert power to complement the power of authority. He must not assume advocacy positions and stifle problem solving behavior. He must only summarize, suggest, and restate alternatives. The behaviors of line managers which are described as strong, quick and decisive would be considered dogmatic, closed-minded, and bull-headed if exhibited by an integrator. Thus selection is one of the organization design variables.

There is some indication that individuals with high needs for affiliation, as measured by TAT's, perform better as integrators than those with low needs for affiliation.[13] While this finding makes some intuitive sense, it also suggests that individuals with high needs for achievement do not perform well as integrators. However, individuals who have both a high need for achievement and a high need for affiliation might be superior integrators. Both needs could be satisfied by working through others successfully.

Another body of personality research is relevant to the selection of individuals for integrating roles.[14] The findings suggest that individuals vary in their ability to stand between two conflicting groups without being absorbed into one of them or accepted by neither of them. The integrator must have credibility with all groups and be seen as unbiased. These are the attributes of the marginal man personality. Predictions from the theory are that marginal men are less dogmatic and more open-minded than other individuals. These theories may be useful in providing a more effective basis for selecting integrators.

A second method for increasing the influence of the integrating role is by increasing the amount of supporting formal information that is available. Usually the information system reports actual expenditures against functional or departmental budgets. The integrator can assume more influence if he can isolate costs and revenues attributable to his decision area—product, program, or unit. He can then identify problems and evaluate alternatives more easily. The organization must maintain a dual information reporting system by summarizing the same information several ways. PERT/cost systems are a typical example of systems which are used to support project managers in guiding projects across functional departments.

Thus the integrator is a formal embodiment of expert power. He exercises influence based on his access to knowledge and information. The role requires the individual to behave in ways that remove possible impediments to information sharing and problem solving. Such individuals are difficult to find and training technologies are not yet developed to create them. Yet this role is becoming increasingly important.

MANAGERIAL LINKING ROLES

The use of an integrating role, like the coordination mechanisms already discussed, has its limitations. These limits are the limitations of expert power. The limitations come into effect when uncertainty and goal diversity increase. We will discuss both of these factors before suggesting the design changes that are required.

When organizations perform highly uncertain tasks and face unique circumstances, there are never enough facts to determine solutions to decision problems. In these circumstances, there is no body of knowledge or valid theory to explain the phenomena in question. Thus there is little basis upon which one can become expert. The leverage of expert power is diminished vis-a-vis the legitimate power of hierarchical position and its complementary reward power. In order to achieve coordination across functional areas, the integrating role requires another source of influence.

A second limitation arises as organizations confront disagreement or uncertainty about ends or goals, rather than means.[15] Admittedly it is difficult to separate ends and means, but there are situations, particularly political situations facing government organizations, in which the inability of participants to agree on a joint decision rests on questions of values rather than lack of knowledge of cause and effect. Busing of school children and redistribution of income are examples of the kind of situation in which expert power is less effective. It is difficult to be an expert on value questions.

Other goal differences stem from the environmental context in which an organization operates. In some government projects which cut across agencies, it is difficult to get joint agreement on funds reallocation from one agency to another. This is because Congress is influenced in its budgeting process by the size of last year's budget. Therefore, any reduction in an agency's funds reduces the likelihood of its getting more in the future. Since the agency is always aware of this fact, the integrator needs more than expert power to reallocate resources among agencies when new information demonstrates a need for reallocation. The accomplishment of organizational goals requires greater integrator influence in decision making. The issue is how to increase the power of the integrator role.

The approach suggested here is that the role become more like a normal managerial role. Influence can be increased by increasing formal position power through a number of changes which are listed below. The role is no longer an integrating role, since its occupant begins to actively enter the decision process. This role is called a managerial linking role for lack of a better label. It is still different from the normal managerial role because the people who perform most of the work for which the linking manager is responsible do not report to him. If people do not work for the linking manager, how does he exercise influence?

1. *Approval Power in Decision Process.*   The first step in increasing the formal power of the linking manager is to put him into the decision process. For example, when departmental budgets are prepared, they can be sent to the linking managers prior to going to the general manager. The linking manager can suggest some interdepartmental tradeoffs which cannot be seen from the local perspective of each department. Subsequent changes to the budget in light of new information must get the approval of the linking manager. This increases the amount of influence that is exercised by the linking manager in the decision process in question. Most of the influence still remains in the departments, however.

2. *Earlier Entrance in Decision and Planning Process.*   The linking manager can have greater influence in the decision process by entering into it at an earlier stage. The earlier one enters into a decision process the greater the effect he can have on the final choice.[16] If one can choose which problems to work on and generate the alternatives to solve them, he has greater influence on the final outcome than the one who merely approves and suggests incremental changes.

The way this concept is put into effect in an organization is to begin the yearly budgeting process with the linking manager and then send his plans to the departments for approval and for checking resource availability. Take for example the linking manager in the hospital: the unit manager. He would forecast activity in his area or ward for the coming year. Then he would prepare resource budgets to carry out the activity. He would do this with the help of the physicians, nurses, dieticians, and service people who work in his ward but do not report to him. Each unit manager would send the plan to the heads of nursing, dietary, services, etc., to see if resources are available; then he would begin to reconcile any resource discrepancies. Similar processes exist for product managers who formulate product strategies and prepare product budgets.

Beginning the planning process with the linking role increases the influence that can be exercised by the role occupant; it allows him to initiate tasks more easily. This does not mean that the linking manager could not initiate changes otherwise, but it does mean it is easier to do so when the formal process begins with him. Before he had to persuade all department heads to change. It was easy for any one of them to say no. It was the linking manager's job to justify why the change should be made. When the linking manager initiates a change formally, it becomes the job of the department head to justify why the change cannot be made. Early entry in the planning and budgeting process makes change initiation a legitimate behavior of the integrator.

The effectiveness of an integrator's (1) having approval authority and (2) entering the planning process depends on his (3) having an adequate information system to support the decision process. These three factors are not alternative ways to supply power to the role. They are complementary and cumulative. The linking manager who does the planning also has approval power and an information system. The extent to which the factors are used depends upon the task uncertainty and priorities of organizational goals.

3. *Budget Control.*   If the linking role requires still more power, it can be given control of the budget for its decision area. The dollars flow through the linking manager into the departments. In effect, the linking manager buys resources from the departments. So after preparing the plan, he receives the budgeted amount of money to gain more control over the use of resources and personnel who do not report to him.

This process has taken place. In aerospace industries, the project manager has received the contracted amount of money for his project. He then purchased the resources, inside the organization and out, to perform the project. He could also reallocate resources during project performance. For example, if it appeared that a device could be actuated electronically, he would buy some resources of the electronics lab. If it later appeared cheaper to actuate the device hydraulically, resources would be shifted from the electronics to the hydraulics laboratory. The lab budgets would be changed accordingly. The laboratories still receive money over which they have control, for independent research and development work, equipment purchase, training, and other activities related to the development of the resources of the lab and have some approval power with respect to project manager decisions on subcontracts and budget changes. Thus the labs are not entirely dependent on project work for funds.

This change gives the linking manager greater influence in the decision process. He becomes more active in it. He becomes a planner, decision maker, and resource allocator. However, none of the resources are his immediate responsibility. He has only information, knowledge, approvals, and money with which to influence the activities in his area of decision. For many organizations, this design is sufficient to guarantee efficient specialization, utilization, and development of resources and at the same time effective integration of specialized resources to maintain product or program integrity. Other organizations require more power in the linking role to effect program integration.

MATRIX ORGANIZATION

Some organizations, or units within an organization, are faced with tasks that require specialized resources in an environment that requires integration of programs. Therefore the organization would like greater integration of specialized resources. It would reject a strategy of organizing resources around self-contained programs, projects, or products, for such a move would either reduce specialization or require duplication of resources. An alternative is to increase the power of the role that champions integration. The integrating role can acquire this power through the establishment of a dual reporting relationship. That is, at some level of the organization, a manager becomes a member of both the resource department and the product or program office. He has two bosses. An example of an aerospace matrix is shown in Figure 16. It shows a project manager and, for very large projects, an assistant project manager. Reporting to the assistant (or, on small- and medium-sized projects, to the project manager) is the subproject manager. He is also a department manager for the laboratory. All the project work in that lab is performed in his department. Therefore he plays the dual role of representing both the project and the laboratory. Above and below him in the structure is the normal single reporting system.

The primary design issue in the matrix is where to establish the dual reporting relation in each laboratory, department, etc. This level is determined mostly by technological determinants of work divisibility. In Figure 16 a departmental package is feasible. All work in that department is for that project. This does not mean that individual scientists and engineers do not work on several projects, however. If there is a fixed departmental structure and the project needs to be worked on in several departments of a lab, there are alternative designs. One is to have the department manager who is responsible for the largest proportion of lab work be the subproject manager. Another is to create an integrating role for the laboratory at a status equivalent to department manager. This

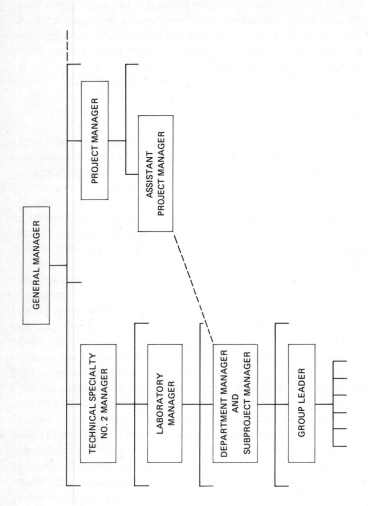

Fig. 16 Formal authority structure of matrix organization.

means that the group leaders will have dual reporting relations as well. They will report to both department managers and subproject managers. For small packages of work, group leaders may function as subproject manager. Thus the size and divisibility of work determine the level at which the dual relation is established.

Drawing a line on an organization chart does not give a person influence, but it does establish some legitimacy. Again referring to Figure 16, we can see that the integrator becomes more influential because his work as department manager is evaluated by both the project manager and the laboratory manager. They jointly determine his chances for promotion and his salary increase, and they determine performance goals with him. This is the mechanism by which more project influence is brought to bear at lower levels of the organization.

The effect of this change is to create a power balance between the roles of department manager and integrator, each of whom champions a different set of goals. In aerospace the project manager encourages performance within budget, on schedule, and within contract specifications. Laboratory managers encourage full utilization of resources, long-run resource development, and highly sophisticated technical performance. For some organizations these goals are of equal importance in general, but they vary in importance in specific instances. Each circumstance, which cannot be predicted in advance, needs to be resolved on its own merits. Rather than refer each circumstance to a general manager, the matrix design institutionalizes an adversary system. The resultant goal conflict implements search behavior to discover current information and to create alternatives to resolve the conflict.

The joint decisions of the adversaries will reflect global considerations to the degree that power is distributed across the roles in proportion to the importance of the subgoals for global goals and to the degree that the role occupant employs behavior which leads to joint problem solving. The power balance is, in a sense, an unachievable razor's edge, but it needs only to be approximated. The power attributable to each role is determined by the selection of the occupant, the design of information systems to support the role, initiation and approval powers in the planning and control process, control of money to effect goals, and the establishment of formal authority relations. In the matrix shown in Figure 16, the laboratory manager and the project manager participate equally in these processes.

If external conditions require still greater program, project, product, or unit integration, the power of the respective managers must be increased further. In some organizations this can be accomplished through symbols of office status. The project managers can be given a higher rank and salary than their peers managing the laboratories. But the final change is to establish sole reporting relationships to the project manager. Thus some of the dual reporting relations are eliminated. This is usually done for when program specialization is less costly than skill specialization; it is done wherever economies of scale and levels of technology are lowest. Thus some of the administrative functions become program-specialized and work for only the program manager. Further establishment of sole reporting relations move the organization toward being a self contained structure. This power continuum will be developed further in the next chapter.

SUMMARY

In this chapter we have articulated a power continuum for integrating and linking roles in organizations. These roles are established to provide program integration when the organization judges self-contained programs to be too costly and when decision making about specific programs overloads the general manager. Then integration through lateral relations may be indicated. The amount of power needed to influence organizational behavior depends on the task uncertainty and the degree to which the organization's environmental context demands program integration. First, in our continuum, only expert power was used. This was controlled by selecting individuals with relevant knowledge and having them behave so as to be at crossroads of information flow. Next, this strategy was strengthened by supporting the role with a formal information system. The next step was to increase power by entering the role in the decision process and thereby creating a managerial role. The managerial linking role entered the decision process first by approval, then by his initiation of the planning process in his area. The next step was to give the linking manager budget control over his area of interest. Further increases in power were established by the creation of dual reporting relations. This entered the linking manager into the reward system in a formal, legitimate manner. The final step was to transfer some resources to the linking manager on a full-time, sole reporting basis. These steps are cumulative. Each is added to the previous powers. The question now becomes one of determining how far along the power continuum one should go. How do you choose? This is the topic of the next chapter.

NOTES

1. The reader should be warned that most of the assertions are based on my informed opinion and working hypotheses. With the exception of *Organization and Environment,* by Paul Lawrence and Jay Lorsch, there is little research to draw upon.
2. Michel Crozier, *The Bureaucratic Phenomenon* (Chicago: University of Chicago Press, 1964), Chapter 6.
3. Paul Lawrence and Jay Lorsch, *Organization and Environment* (Boston: Division of Research, Harvard Business School, 1967).
4. *Ibid.,* p. 11.
5. *Ibid.,* Chapter 1.
6. *Ibid.,* Chapter 2.
7. *Ibid.,* Chapter 2.
8. *Ibid.,* Chapter 3.
9. James G. March and Herbert Simon, *Organizations* (New York: John Wiley, 1958), pp. 164–166.
10. *Ibid.,* p. 165.
11. Norman R. F. Maier, "Assets and Liabilities in Group Problem Solving: The Need for an Integrative Function," *Psychological Review* **74** (4), 239–249 (1967).
12. *Ibid.,* p. 246.
13. Paul Lawrence and Jay Lorsch, "New Management Job: The Integrator," *Harvard Business Review,* November-December 1967, pp. 142–151.
14. R. C. Ziller, B. J. Stark, and H. O. Pruden, "Marginality and Integrative Management Positions," *Academy of Management Journal,* December 1969, pp. 487–495.
15. James D. Thompson and Arthur Tuden, "Strategies, Structures and Processes of Organizational Decision," in James D. Thompson et al. (eds.), *Comparative Studies in Administration* (Pittsburgh: University of Pittsburgh Press, 1959), pp. 195–216.
16. James D. Thompson and William J. McEwen, "Organizational Goals and Environment: Goal Setting as an Interaction Process," *American Sociological Review,* February 1958, pp. 23–31.

Chapter 8
REVIEW OF MODEL AND EMPIRICAL EVIDENCE

The four organization design strategies have been presented in their entirety. This chapter briefly reviews the entire framework. Then some empirical evidence and further clarifications are discussed, particularly with reference to lateral relations. The remaining chapters present case examples and discuss some operational problems with lateral relations.

THE FRAMEWORK IN REVIEW

The theory underlying the framework was based on the premise that observed variations in organization form represent variations in the strategies of organizations to adapt to information processing requirements. In order to establish this premise, it was necessary to identify information processing requirements, to explain how organizations process information, to identify the strategies, and to explore the conditions under which the strategies would be chosen.

The information processing requirements facing an organization were primarily related to the degree of task uncertainty, which was defined as the difference between the amount of information required to coordinate cooperative action and the amount of information actually possessed by the organization. The amount of information required was a function of the output diversity, the division of labor, and the level of performance. The greater each of these factors were, the greater the number of factors that had to be considered simultaneously in order to reach decisions. If the organization did not possess the information, then it had to be acquired during the execution of the task. Thus it was postulated that a critical limiting factor of organizational form was the capacity of the organization to process information and make decisions during the actual execution of a task.

To explain how information processing limited the form of the organization, the basic mechanistic bureaucratic model was created. The model started with a large task in which the work was divided up on the basis of input skill specialization. The design problem arises because the behavior that occurs in one of these subtasks cannot be judged as good or bad except in relation to the behaviors occurring in other subtasks. The behaviors must be coordinated, but in an organization of any size, each employee cannot possibly communicate with all the others with whom he is interdependent. The design problem is to create mechanisms that permit coordinated action across large numbers of interdependent roles. Each of the mechanisms has a range over which it is effective. The mechanisms were discussed by starting with low-level information processing (a predictable task) and increasing the amount of information by increasing task uncertainty.

In the basic bureaucratic model, some behaviors were determined by rules created beforehand and communicated to role occupants, others were determined by the role occupant in accordance with limited goals and targets, and still others were decided by managers in the hierarchy after an unanticipated event occurred. The upward referral process, which was needed to generate decisions when exceptional events occurred, became overloaded as highly uncertain tasks generated large numbers of exceptions. The organization could then choose from among four strategies. Two of them reduced interdependence among the roles and reduced the need to process information, while two others created mechanisms to process more information.

Alternative 1: Creation of slack resources reduced the level of performance. Lower performance reduced the interdependence between roles and made it unnecessary to consider large numbers of decision factors simultaneously. Since there are many dimensions to performance, the design problem was to find the one that would reduce the overload and for which lower performance would be acceptable among the organization's clients, suppliers, owners, etc.

Alternative 2: Creation of self-contained units occurred when groups of input resources were devoted solely to one output category. By making all resource groups self-contained, there was no need to process information about resource sharing among outputs and, because of reduced division of labor, less need to coordinate roles. Like slack resources, self-contained units reduced interdependence, making it unnecessary to simultaneously consider a large number of factors in decision making. The design choices were to select the basis of self-containment, the degree of self-containment, and the level at which the self-contained groups would report.

Alternative 3: Investment in the vertical information system expanded the capacity of hierarchical channels of communication, created new ones, and increased the capacity of decision mechanisms. The chief mechanism was the utilization of new information technologies and computers. The design variables were the frequency of decision making, the scope of the data base available to the decision mechanism, the capacity of the decision mechanism, and the degree of formalization of language to be used in communicating about events which the organization faced.

Alternative 4: Creation of lateral relations selectively implemented communication channels across lines of authority. These channels need to be designed, because the "informal organization" did not spontaneously arise to coordinate interdependencies not encompassed by the hierarchy of authority. The lateral processes are listed below in a sequence determined by increasing ability to handle information and increasing cost to the organization.

1. *Direct contact* between managers
2. Creation of *liaison role*
3. Creation of *task forces*
4. Use of *teams*
5. Creation of *integrating role*
6. Change to *managerial linking role*
7. Establishing the *matrix form*

There are several design questions associated with each of these mechanisms, but they will not be repeated here.

It was hypothesized that as organizations take on tasks of increasing uncertainty, they must choose one or some combination of these strategies in order to cope with increased information processing. If they did not consciously choose, then it is hypothesized that slack is automatically generated in order to balance the information processing requirements of the task and the capacity of the organization to process information.

There is some evidence to support these assertions. In the remainder of this chapter some empirical studies are presented. In the following chapter, two case studies are discussed in greater detail.

LATERAL RELATIONS AND INFLUENCE DISTRIBUTION

The use of lateral relations, which begin with direct contact and run through the matrix design, significantly alters the distribution of power in an organization's decision processes. In part, the distribution is a reflection of task uncertainty and, in part, a reflection of environmental influences. The effect of uncertainty is demonstrated in the findings of Lawrence and Lorsch[1] (see Table II). The data shown are taken from

Table II

	Plastics	Food	Container
% New products in last 20 years	35%	15%	0%
Integrating devices	Rules	Rules	Rules
	Hierarchy	Hierarchy	Hierarchy
	Goal setting	Goal setting	Goal setting
	Direct contact	Direct contact	Direct contact
	Teams at 3 levels	Task forces	
	Integrating Dept.	Integrators	
% Integrators/ managers	22%	17%	0%

the most effective divisions of firms in three different industries. The industries differ in the amount of new product activity they have undertaken. It is assumed that increased product activity increases the degree of task uncertainty. The comparison therefore holds effectiveness constant and high and varies the degree of task uncertainty. The extent to which lateral relations are used varies directly with the degree of task uncertainty. The container company works effectively through the hierarchy with a minimum of formal, lateral contacts. Alternatively, the uncertain tasks facing the plastics firm requires extensive use of lateral relations in order to resolve the uncertainties. The fact that extensive lateral relations are more costly is reflected by the proportion of managers who perform integrating roles in integrating departments. The cost of lateral relations, more management personnel, is quite clear.

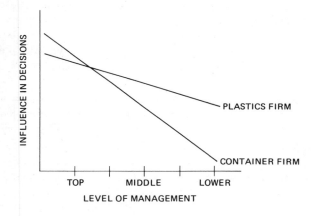

Fig. 17 Hierarchical distribution of influence.

The effect of lateral relations on the vertical distribution of influence is shown graphically in Figure 17. The successful container firm has proportionally more influence concentrated at the top, whereas the plastics firm has a more even distribution. The effect of task uncertainty is to overload the top levels in the plastics firm, necessitating the decentralization of decisions. The combination of Table II and Figure 17 indicates that the decentralization takes place through the establishment of lateral relations. It also illustrates that decentralization is not good or bad *per se* but depends on the level of task uncertainty.

Task uncertainty also affects the horizontal distribution of influence. Every organization requires the coordination of specialized resources. Uncertainty has the effect of making prior decisions inadequate. Decisions must then be made in light of current information. Many of these decisions require the global perspective of the general manager. However, uncertainty also has the effect of overloading the general management role. As decisions are pushed down to lower levels, the general manager controls the decision process by controlling the power bases of the participants in joint decisions. As uncertainty increases, more decisions about integrating resources around outputs are made at lower levels. Therefore, the role that champions product, unit, or program integration requires more power as uncertainty increases. The increase is obtained by the use of lateral relations and the power factors described in the previous chapter. Actually, there is a continuum of relative power in the decision process; it varies from a predominantly resource-based structure, like the container firm, all the way to a self-contained, program-based structure.

This continuum is shown in Figure 18. The extent to which lateral relations and the power factors are used determines where a particular organization is located along the bottom line. The diagram shows the power distribution for the product vs. function choice for a manufacturing firm. It could be project-function or function-geographic area as well. Starting on the far left, the decision making influence is strictly functional. If the firm wishes to bring more product orientation into its decision process, it introduces product task forces, product teams, and then integrators (product managers). In so doing it moves along the bottom line toward the right.

In the previous chapter, the movement from a functional structure to a matrix was described. The movement could have been continued by having all departments report to the original integrating position. But now the functional manager becomes the integrator. He works for the goal of resource integrity across a product-divisionalized structure. Similarly, there can be functional teams and functional task forces. Indeed a scenario could have been created, starting with product departments

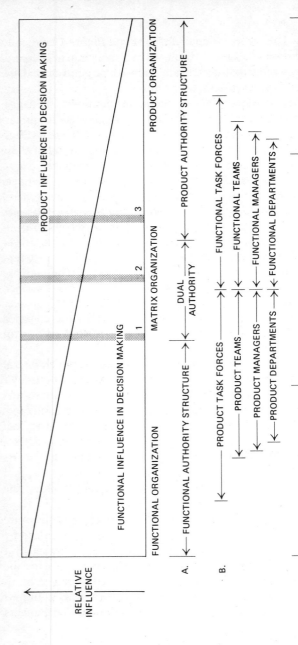

Fig. 18 The range of alternatives. (From Jay Galbraith, "Designing Matrix Organizations," *Business Horizons*, February 1971.)

and subjecting the organization to changes in technology, requiring more specialized resources.

Research on organizations has not progressed to a point where an organization can locate where it should be on the diagram. But the research does allow us to determine the major factors to which we can add our subjective weightings. In addition, we can locate our present position and make changes in the appropriate directions as the factors change. This provides a basis for planning the organization, along with plans for strategy and resource allocation.

What factors should we consider when choosing the distribution and direction of influence? Most of the research pertains to industrial organizations, but with substitutions of appropriate categories the results can be applied to noncommercial organizations as well. The first factors are the effects of uncertainty and diversity. For industrial organizations, these factors are indicated rates of market change, rate of new product introduction, and diversity of product lines. Some of the relevant research has already been presented.[2] The greater the rate of new product introduction, the greater the use of lateral relations and the greater the influence of the product manager. These same results are replicated in a larger study of 397 business firms.[3]

> Most significantly, businesses with program organizations seem to have been considerably more successful in developing and introducing new products than businesses without program organizations. For example 36.9% of the 358 businesses which had product program managers reported that more than 20% of 1967 sales were accounted for by new products, while only 19.8% of the businesses without product program managers made this claim.[4]

Similarly, a diversity of product lines tends to overload the decision process of functional organizations. In the introduction this pressure was shown to lead to the establishment of product divisions. For a small organization or when a division itself diversifies, the same pressures exist but the costs of divisionalization are too great. Therefore they undertake lateral relations and establish product integrators. The results of one study were summarized as follows:

> There was a striking relationship between the amount of product and/or market diversity faced by a business and its use of program

managers. In all industry and size classifications, the more diversified a business's products and/or markets, the more likely it was to
have a program structure.[5]

Thus uncertainty and diversity create decision overloads which force the
introduction of integrating roles. One study of hospitals reports a higher
proportion of administrative staff in general hospitals than in specialized
tuberculosis hospitals.[6] While the study does not identify the kinds of
roles in the structure, it shows that there is a relation between the
diversity of diseases and ills served and the number of managers required
to provide the service. When combined with the Lawrence and Lorsch
findings, the hospital study supports the generality of the information
overload theory.

A second factor associated with the use of lateral relations and
integrating roles is subtask interdependence. Using a longitudinal case
study approach, Galbraith illustrates the increase in use of lateral relations after the time allowed for new product introduction was reduced.[7]
The case is explained more fully in the next chapter.

The findings from the Sloan School Project on the Management of
Science and Technology help put the discussion in perspective.[8] If tight
schedules, uncertainty, and diversity were the only forces operating,
lateral relations would give way to self-contained program organizations.
But the data from aerospace firms performing high technology projects
for the government reveal that firms with technical personnel organized
on a functional basis produce projects that are technically superior to
those produced by firms that organize technical personnel on a project
basis. Better technical performance is associated with resource-based
organization forms. The same study also reveals that firms organizing
administrative personnel on a project basis and firms using PERT information systems are more likely to meet their cost and schedule targets.
Therefore, in order to create high technology on tight schedules, the firm
should use a matrix with technical personnel organized on a functional
basis and with a project office containing administrative personnel supported by a project-related information system.

Current evidence thus supports the theory being developed here.
Increases in uncertainty, diversity, and performance exert pressures to
move the organization to the right in Figure 18. Increases in specialization and economies of scale exert forces to move the organization to the
left. Where the organization should be depends on the sum of these

factors. When opposing forces are equally strong, the matrix design results.

All these studies indicate the direction of change. They indicate use of lateral relations and integrating roles. But the data are not precise enough to specify exact power distributions. The evidence is inconclusive about the power and influence of the integrating role. For example, Lawrence and Lorsch find all integrators have high influence, and so they cannot distinguish between successful and unsuccessful performance on that basis.[9] Similarly, Marquis could find no relationship between project performance and the types and amounts of influence a project manager had.[10] The paucity of results is partly due to the difficulty of measuring power and influence as opposed to measuring the existence of a role and the number of people performing in it.

Some anecdotal evidence is available, however, on changes in power distribution in aerospace firms over a period of time. In addition to illustrating power shifts, our example highlights the effect of environmental context on internal influence processes. Recall that in aerospace, tradeoffs were made between project technical performance, schedule completion, and cost. These general managerial decisions were decentralized to become joint decisions between a laboratory or functional manager championing technical performance and resource utilization, and a project manager championing schedule completion and project cost.

In the late 1950's and early 1960's, technical performance was the critical dimension. The environment was characterized by Sputnik, the space race, and the missile gap. It was deemed imperative by the government to produce technical accomplishments and to do it rapidly. The priorities ran technical performance first, schedule second, and cost a poor third. Data on actual performance during this time period reflect this order of priorities.[11] All projects met or exceeded technical specifications, but completion times were 1.5 times as great as projected, and costs exceeded targets by a factor of 3.2. In aerospace firms performing these projects, the functional managers dominated the joint decisions, but project managers were also influential due to time pressures. Since technical performance dominated, the influence distribution was approximated by the dotted line (1) in Figure 18.

In the early and middle 1960's the environment changed. This was the McNamara era. He was of the opinion that technical performance could be achieved but at less cost. The contracts changed from cost plus fixed fee to various incentive contracts and fixed price contracts. Defense department officials demanded that aerospace firms use PERT, then PERT/Cost information systems. The effect of these changes was to make the project manager more influential in the decision process. In Figure 18 the influence distribution was represented by the dotted line (2).

Still another change occurred in the late 1960's. Strong pressures to reduce defense costs began operating. First there was the publicity concerning cost overruns on the giant C-5 A aircraft. Senator Proxmire began hearings on contractor efficiency practices. Finally, inflation and shifting national priorities all combined to make cost the top priority as opposed to technical performance and schedule completion. In the internal workings of aerospace firms, the project managers began to dominate the joint decision processes. The influence pattern was explicit. Project managers held vice-presidential status whereas laboratory and functional managers had the title of "director." The influence distribution moved to line (3) in Figure 18.

Currently, still another change is occurring. The national government is shifting spending away from aerospace projects. The effect is to reduce the size of the aerospace industry and firms in it. The firms must retain specialized personnel to create the technology, but at the same time, they are forced to reduce costs and size. Thus effective utilization of specialized resources across a number of projects has increased in importance. Firms must avoid duplication of personnel or fractional utilization of shared resources. Internally the functional managers are regaining some of their previous strengths, in order to increase utilization. Reduced size increases the importance of the utilization of resources and of its champion, the resource manager.

This brief account of the aerospace industry demonstrates how environmental influences affect internal decision processes. Normally, the general manager would watch these trends and alter his decision making behavior accordingly. But when decisions are decentralized, the general managers must change internal power bases in addition to his own decision behavior. It becomes the task of the general manager to see that the distribution of internal influence reflects the external realities that the organization faces. He must take an open system view of the organization.

A similar sequence of events has taken place in hospitals over a longer period of time.[12] Decision making in hospitals revolves around the triumvirate of trustees, doctors, and administration. Originally, hospitals for the most part served those members of the community who could not afford treatment in their homes. Therefore, the hospital depended on the trustees to donate their own money and to secure donations from the community to finance its operations. The technological advances represented by sophisticated equipment for treatment and diagnosis shifted power to the medical staff, because they were the only ones trained to understand the resources needed by the hospital. Also more patients were treated in hospitals than in their homes. The hospitals became financially dependent upon the physicians who referred patients to them. Trustees were still influential because financing was required for the acquisition of the sophisticated equipment. Recently there has been a shift in power escalating the influence of the administrative staff. Increases in specialization and demands for complete utilization of facilities make the administrator and unit manager more active in the coordination of activities. There is also an increase in external interdependence. The hospital needs to coordinate its activities with other health agencies in the community. The administrative staff have external contacts, which enable them to influence external affairs to aid internal problems in the hospital. It is important for organizations to adapt to these realities. Those hospitals and aerospace firms which adapted first were the most successful. Those institutions which cannot achieve the internal power shifts are those which are most likely to fail.

Thus as patterns of interdependence, task uncertainty, diversity, and external conditions change, the organization must change its decision making structure in order to remain effective.

It should be mentioned that this analysis assumes that the organization must adapt to its environment. In some cases, they must. However, there are other occasions when the organization can change the environment rather than adapt to the environment. This possibility is not discussed here.[13]

NOTES

1. Paul Lawrence and Jay Lorsch, *Organization and Environment* (Boston: Harvard Business School, 1967), Chapter 6.
2. Lawrence and Lorsch, *op. cit.;* and Tom Burns and G. M. Stalker, *Management and Innovation* (London: Tavistock, 1958).
3. E. Raymond Corey and Steven H. Star, *Organization Strategy: A Marketing*

Approach (Boston: Division of Research, Harvard Business School, 1970), Chapter 6.

4. *Ibid.,* p. 54.

5. *Ibid.,* p. 52.

6. Theodore Anderson and Seymour Warkov, "Organizational Size and Functional Complexity: A Study of Administration in Hospitals," *American Sociological Review,* February 1961, pp. 23–28.

7. Jay Galbraith, "Environmental and Technological Determinants of Organization Design," in Jay Lorsch and Paul Lawrence (eds.), *Studies in Organization Design* (Homewood, Ill.: Richard D. Irwin, 1970), pp. 113–139.

8. Donald Marquis, "Ways of Organizing Projects," *Innovation,* No. 5, 1969, pp. 26–33.

9. Lawrence and Lorsch, *op. cit.,* p. 62.

10. D. G. Marquis and D. M. Straight, "Organizational Factors in Project Performance," Sloan School of Management Working Paper No. 133–65, M.I.T., August 1965.

11. Peck and Sherer, *The Weapons Acquisition Process* (Boston: Division of Research, Harvard Business School, 1962).

12. Charles Perrow, "The Analysis of Goals in Complex Organizations," *American Sociological Review* **26** (1961), 854–866; and Charles Perrow, "Hospitals: Technology, Structure and Goals," in James G. March, *Handbook of Organizations* (Chicago: Rand-McNally, 1965), Chapter 22.

13. See Jay R. Galbraith, *Organization Design* (Reading, Mass.: Addison-Wesley), forthcoming.

Chapter 9
CASE STUDIES

The entire framework and some supporting evidence have now been presented. Some examples have been given throughout to illustrate specific points. In this chapter two case studies will be presented. They are intended to highlight the trade-offs articulated in the theory and also to demonstrate practical usefulness.

RESPONSE TO A MARKET CHANGE

The history of the Commercial Airplane Division of the Boeing Company can be used to illustrate the design choices that have been derived in the theory.[1] The Commercial Airplane Division is responsible for the generation, design, and production of aircraft for many of the world's airlines. The organization is shown in Figure 19. It reflects a product-divisionalized structure with functional integrating departments. After experiencing substantial growth and introducing new models in the early 1960's, the Commercial Airplane Division reorganized to the divisionalized form. This change illustrates the effect of diversity and size on an organization. However, since all product branches were concentrated in the Seattle area and most labor markets were tight, the functional integrating departments were influential in manpower allocation. Our inter-

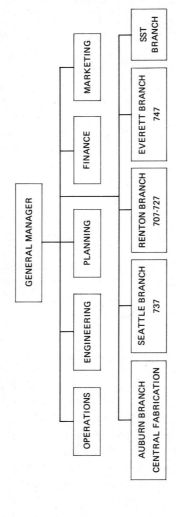

Fig. 19 Organization chart of the Commercial Airplane Division.

est concentrates on the product branch organization which designs and produces a single type of aircraft.

Coordination in a Product Branch

A typical product branch organization is shown in Figure 20. The branch employed about 10,000 people and produced about ten aircraft a month. Each aircraft required about 14 months to two years for completion. The branch engaged in the sequential process of design of product, design of the process, acquisition and fabrication of parts, assembly of parts, and finally testing and delivery. Invariably the branches chose the functional form illustrated in Figure 20.

The functional form placed the design of the aircraft in a unit under a single authority structure. This was done because the design process involves uncertain and reciprocally interdependent activities of the highest priority. The design had to meet the specifications guaranteed to the airlines and meet the safety requirements of the government or there would be no sales. Thus the activities which were most difficult to coordinate were also the most consequential. The product design unit was structured so as to coordinate the design activities most effectively. Similarly, purchasing and manufacturing were functional so as to exploit common vendor groupings and economies of scale in equipment and tooling, respectively.

The effect of the functional organization was to create for the branch manager the problem of coordinating the sequential workflow between the functions. The mechanism for coordination is a schedule which provides targets for each function to guide its completion of the work. The schedule must allow each function enough time to do its work and still complete the work in the time desired by the customer. The task of scheduling is a problem of considerable magnitude both within and between the interdependent functions. Let us analyze how this scheduling function was performed in one of the branches.

1. *Functional Integrating Departments.* The two primary functions, product design and manufacturing, each had its own integrating department which was responsible for scheduling between the other departments within its own function. The cost and schedules group in product design served this function by collecting detailed information for decisions concerning technical performance, cost, and schedule completion.

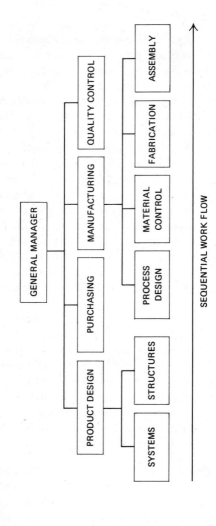

Fig. 20 Functional organization of a product branch—before change.

The scheduling function in manufacturing scheduled the flow of some 100,000 parts into final assembly. Those were the locations of information concerning schedules and status of operations. Therefore a good deal of the scheduling was decentralized within the two primary functions.

The functional scheduling departments handled the sequential interdependence within the functions but did not solve the problem of coordinating sequential interdependence between functions. The manner in which this coordination was carried out varied with the type of decision. One mechanism established the original schedule for each airplane and other mechanisms handled deviations from it.

2. *Branch Integrating Department.* An overall schedule was established for each aircraft upon its order. This schedule was determined by a team of representatives from product design, manufacturing, purchasing, division marketing, and a customer representative. An integrator, called a program manager, served as chairman of this team in order to achieve a schedule in the best interest of the branch. He was the representative of the branch general manager. Negotiations began by having the manufacturing scheduling representative work backward from the date desired by the customer and by having product design's cost and schedules representative work forward from the present. The aim was to achieve a set of milestones that everyone could live with. These milestones then guided subsequent scheduling within the individual functions.

The program manager's integrating department was responsible for getting the schedule established and monitoring schedule progress, but only in an aggregate way. They provided information for the general manager's review of major milestones, rather than detailed information to guide the scheduling effort.

This method of coordination worked very well as long as every department met its due date, or milestone. It is only when due dates are missed and missed in substantial numbers that additional coordination effort is needed. There are two possible types of schedule disruption which require additional resources—predictable and unpredictable causes. Different mechanisms are used in each case.

3. *Change Board.* Predictable disruptions result from the constant flow of design changes from product design engineers. The design changes are caused by attempts to update technology, by rejects from quality control, by liaison engineers, and by customer requests. Since

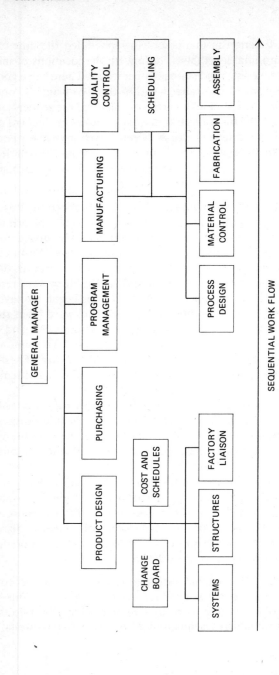

Fig. 21 Typical product branch before change.

design changes are originated in the product design step, the change can have effects on all subsequent functional activity. The additional coordination effort took the form of a team called a change board. Each functional department, including sales had a permanent representative on the board. It was chaired and run by the representative from product design. The board met daily to discuss schedule and budget changes. The changes were then communicated to the affected groups and the functional scheduling departments. All these integrating positions are indicated in Figure 21.

4. *Slack Resources.*   Unpredictable schedule disruptions usually arise due to uncertainties inherent in the task of designing and manufacturing airplanes. The uncertainty varies between functions. The design groups have the greatest uncertainty. The uncertainty also varies with the maturity of the project and the state of the art of the design. Thus the introduction of new models introduces the greatest uncertainty. What makes the problem difficult is that schedule disruptions are most likely to occur in the design functions which are at the start of the sequential work flow. Therefore they can potentially disrupt all subsequent activity.

During the mature stages of a program these disruptions can be handled by scheduling-rescheduling decisions within the functions, by direct contact between affected managers, by informal task force activity, and with the slack that has been built into the schedule. However, when a new model was introduced, the increase in uncertainty overloaded the decision process. The response was to absorb the uncertainty with slack and perform the scheduling less effectively. This was because the uncertainty was temporary and the primary problem was achieving an effective high quality design. The effect of uncertainty on the organization is depicted graphically in Figure 22. It shows the stockout history of the Commercial Airplane Division. A stockout occurs if a part or assembly is not available in the assembly line at its scheduled time. Periods of high stockout activity coincided perfectly with the introduction of new models. These peak periods were tolerated as transient. Indeed, in periods of stability, the system functioned well. It was cheaper to absorb uncertainty with slack than to apply more coordination effort.

In summary, the branches operated a functional organization in order to coordinate the primary subtask of designing the aircraft. This created a problem of sequential interdependence between functions. A schedule to coordinate the sequential activities was established by an

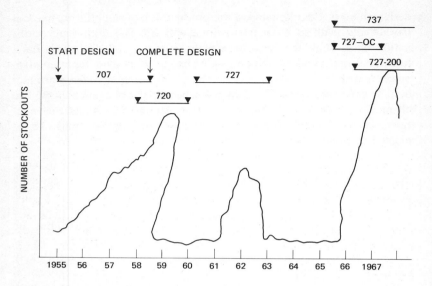

Fig. 22 Stockout history of the Commercial Airplane Division.

interfunctional team chaired by the program manager, an integrating role. The schedule was subsequently elaborated, implemented, and controlled through integrating departments within the functions. Another interfunctional team, the change board, coordinated many of the subsequent design changes; it was chaired by product design. Finally, slack was used to reduce the magnitude of the task, particularly at times of new model introduction. Thus scheduling was decentralized and controlled within the two principal functions.

Environmental Changes

In the years 1963 to 1966, some significant environmental changes took place. First, there was an enormous increase in the demand for commercial jet aircraft. This required a rapid buildup of men, material, and facilities. Previous buildups at Boeing had been financed by the government, either by progress payments prior to actual delivery of the aircraft or by using government equipment and facilities. Prior to the 747, airlines did not make progress payments. Therefore, the buildup had to be internally financed. The shift from government to commercial markets combined with rapid growth to make cost and financial factors higher in priority.

The other major change occurred in the market. Prior to the middle sixties, the problem in aircraft sales was to demonstrate the profitability of jet over propeller-driven aircraft on commercial routes. The problem was to create a market. In this environment the cost of time and delay is small relative to a mistake in design or construction. Thus prior to making commitments to the airlines on the 707, Boeing built, flew, and tested a prototype. The success of the 707 brought imitation from Douglas in the DC-8 and Convair in the 880. These models were directly competitive for the same airline routes. The same market problem prevailed in introducing the 727. Boeing had to demonstrate the profitability of jets on medium range routes. However, this time they did not build a prototype. Instead, they undertook four years of wind tunnel testing and product development to perfect the three aft-mounted engine design. The 727 was also successful, but this time Douglas did not imitate. They introduced the DC-9 for short-range routes.

After 1964 the problem facing Boeing was not to establish a market but to meet the opportunities remaining as quickly as possible. They introduced the short-range 737, new versions of the 727, the giant 747, and the SST. But each of these received competitive time pressure from the DC-9, an elongated DC-9, an elongated DC-8, the DC-10, Lockheed's L1011, a possible commercial derivative of Lockheed's C-5A, and the British-French Concorde. Now a delay of a few months would result in cancelled orders and fewer sales. The cost of using slack time to uncouple sequentially interdependent subtasks was prohibitive. Thus Boeing operated under compressed schedules. The product development effort which preceded the final design effort was reduced from four years on the 727 to four months on the 747. This left considerable uncertainty to be resolved by the branches in the design stage, while at the same time compressed schedules gave them less time in which to do it.

As the theory would predict, information overloads occurred. The amount of stockout activity shown in Figure 23 during 1966–1967 was higher than at any time in the past. During this same period, stockouts slowed production and caused a financial crisis at the Douglas Company.

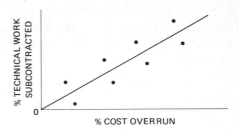

 Fig. 23 Cost overrun history
vs. amount of design
subcontracted.

These facts caused the Boeing management to search for alternative
solutions to the organization design problem.

Organization Design Strategies

The increased task uncertainty (caused by less prior product development work) and interdependence (caused by compressed schedules) in
producing the 747 increased the amount of information that had to be
processed during the actual design and manufacture. Therefore, according to the theory, branches had to undertake some organization design
action. This need was illustrated by the increase in stockouts before any
action was taken. Therefore, the policy to do nothing was tantamount
to a decision to use slack. Not to decide is to decide on slack. But as
stockouts increased and Douglas developed similar problems, Boeing
searched for alternatives.

The theory developed here identifies four alternatives. The first,
slack resources, cannot be used, indeed slack must be reduced. Alternatively, information processing between decision makers could be reduced
by creating self-contained units within the branch. These units could be
formed around the major units which come together to form the aircraft,
such as wing, cab, tail, and body. This alternative was not chosen for two
reasons. First, the critical problem was one of product design. The design
process had the greatest uncertainty, greatest amount of interdependence, and greatest consequence for overall performance of the aircraft.
Splitting up the interdependent units would jeopardize the technical
integration. There is some factual basis for this. A study by engineering
showed that when the design work was subcontracted and performed at
a remote site, that work was more likely to overrun its cost and schedules. Figure 23 shows that the greater the percentage of contracted

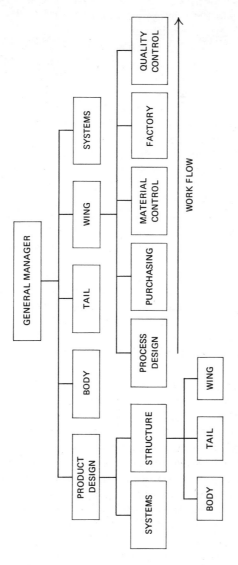

Fig. 24 Product branch with sequentially interdependent clusters.

design work, the greater the percent cost overrun of the original target. Thus for the consequential design work, it is more effective to collocate designers and maintain them in a single structure.

There is also the possibility of placing the design work in one unit and placing the remaining sequential interdependence in self-contained units. This plan would place scheduling, manufacturing, and testing in autonomous units. Such an organization is represented in Figure 24. It was predicted that this change would have been effective in reducing stockouts and providing the decentralized, quick response necessitated by compressed schedules. This design alternative was not chosen, however, because the problem it solved was too transient and temporary to merit a change in overall structure. Figure 22 shows that this problem exists only in the initial stages of a program. In mature stages, the functional organization and previous coordination devices will be appropriate. Therefore, other design alternatives had to be sought which would increase the capacity of the organization to process the information which temporarily overloaded the branch. The responses varied with the program.

1. *Task Forces.*   The primary response of the branches introducing the 737 and various 727 derivatives was to introduce task forces to provide interfunctional coordination. Since the structure could not be changed as indicated in Figure 24, task forces were formed around the major sections. These groups worked the sequential interdependence between functions.

The task forces were able to collect information on an informal basis by walking through the plant and telephoning managers. This interfunctional information, which was not available anywhere else, gave them the basis for setting priorities. The information collected and displayed by the program manager was interfunctional, but not detailed enough or current enough to help set priorities as problems arose. Since the groups in the task forces were responsible for relatively independent tasks, they were able to collect detailed, current information and respond to problems immediately. Also, by spending a good deal of time in the plant, they were able to work with people who had the most knowledge about the problems.

All personnel assigned to the task forces worked full time until the first six to ten aircraft were completed. They were then assigned elsewhere.

The task forces were temporary patchwork on a functional structure which was vulnerable to sequential interdependence. They were a temporary structural change which modified the authority relationship during periods of high uncertainty. During the period of new design introduction, the task force set priorities. Since they had information which cut across functions and were not identified with any single function, they were in a better position to determine priorities than were the functional managers. The functional managers still made decisions relating to who would do the work and how to do it. During periods of task certainty, the functional managers did not need priorities other than "follow the schedule!" But during a new model introduction, the assumptions on which the schedule is based often prove wrong as problems arise. Then the information collecting activities of the task force place them in a position to set new priorities. As the task becomes more predictable, the schedule becomes a more reliable priority device and the task force is not needed.

The task force represents additional coordination effort and cost. It is used in addition to, not instead of, the normal means of coordination. In this case it was used to replace the slack time that had been removed from the schedule.

2. *Liaison.*   Another vulnerable spot in the functional organization is between the product and process design groups. It is here that the uncertainties are highest and there is reciprocal and sequential interdependence. At Boeing, the additional coordination was performed by a liaison group of process designers who were physically stationed in the product design area. Their first responsibility was to work with the product designer and suggest design alternatives which allowed less costly manufacturing processes. Due to environmental changes, the interdependence between these groups required communication and interaction to achieve the necessary coordination. This is true for several reasons. First, the interdependence was not completely worked out in product development. Second, the amount of communication exceeded the capacity of direct managerial contact. The increased volume of activity brought in new engineers who were not familiar with past practices. These factors combined to create a need for liaison engineers.

The liaison group also aided in the coordination of sequential interdependence. If the product designers were late in completing a design, they delayed the start of the process design activity. In order to put a part back on schedule, the process design group would have to resort to overtime. However, the liaison men took advantage of the fact that a part design does not have to be 100% complete before the process design can begin. The tool design can be started if only rough dimensions and material are known. Thus the liaison engineers keep the process designers supplied with work by bringing them partially completed parts designs. In this way the design efforts are run in parallel rather than in series, with the liaison man as the communication link.

Thus the liaison group facilitates mutual adjustment and allows the removal of slack time from the schedule without causing disruptions. The liaison group also represents an increase in coordination costs since it is used in addition to, not instead of, the schedule and direct managerial contact. However, once the design of the new aircraft is complete, the liaison men resume normal duties as process designers or liaison men elsewhere. The activity is needed only in periods of high uncertainty. On some programs this was not a new approach, on others it was. However, on all programs there were both more liaison engineers and higher quality engineers assigned than in the past.

Thus the reduction in slack resources was countered by allocating more resources, liaison and task forces, to coordination through lateral relations. These resources were placed at critical spots in the sequential flow being coordinated by a functional organization. The lateral relations allowed a temporary decentralization of influence. The organization was still a functionally dominant one, but with an integrating role between functions.

The 747 Program

The introduction of the 747 represented one of the largest private undertakings ever attempted. The magnitude of the coordination task rendered the previous mechanisms insufficient. The program still used rules, hierarchy, goal setting and planning, and direct contact. It made extensive use of liaison, task forces, and teams. The departments working on the same section of the aircraft were physically located together. This enhanced the probability that direct contact and informal task forces and teams would develop spontaneously. But more attention needed to be given to the costs incurred and the schedule completion. The means by which this was accomplished was an organization change and a lateral shift in influence. These changes increased the influence of the integrator

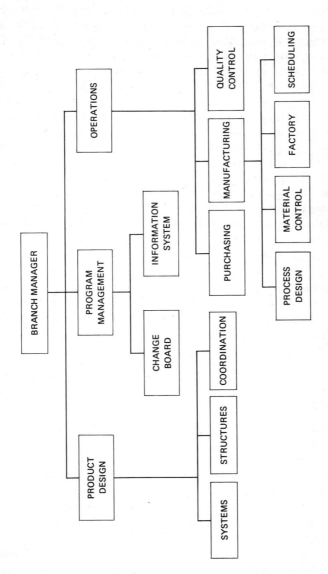

Fig. 25 Product branch organization responsible for 747.

—the program management office. The modified organization is shown in Figure 25.

1. *Structure Change.*   The change in structure had two effects. The first involved the creation of an operations manager. The structure now represented a more inclusive first-order grouping of the sequentially interdependent functions which take place after product design. The second-order grouping consisted of coupling the reciprocally interdependent design units with the sequentially interdependent operations functions. This created two self-contained units which encompassed the major coordination problems. However it still left the problem of coupling product design and operations. To accomplish this, the influence of the program office was increased.

The influence was increased by shifting the change board activity to the program office and enlarging the number of boards operating. The effect of the change was to change the goal orientation of the board chairman to one which was responsive to cost and schedules as well as technical considerations.

2. *Information System.*   The other major change was in the vertical information system. It took the form of an increase in the detail of global information and an increase in the currency of information utilized in the program office. Previously the information in the program office was used more for ex-post evaluation than for ex-ante decision making. Detailed, real-time, interfunctional information for decision making had to be acquired informally by the task forces. The change created a more formalized information system to provide such data. The formalization was accomplished by utilizing a PERT-like network diagram for planning and control purposes. The cost of the change was a large increase in clerical personnel to process the information.

Thus the increase in task uncertainty and tighter coupling of functions was countered with more information and an increased decision making capability. It was easy to change from this design to one required for stable operations. Under the present system, as uncertainty is decreased, the amount of information is decreased. The frequency of reporting can be reduced from daily to weekly, weekly to bi-weekly. The PERT system will not be needed. The number of information processing people can be decreased to a normal level as the task certainty increases. Although the form of coordination is different, its intensity still varies directly with the uncertainty of the task.

The case study described is intended to illustrate the framework developed in the book and to highlight the trade-off between slack, authority structure, vertical information systems, and lateral relations. The example first described the mechanisms the organization used to come to terms with its environment. Then as the environment changed, the organization had to adjust its mechanisms of coordination. Whether these changes were effective is clearly a matter of conjecture. However, it is possible to claim that they were effective. Boeing, at the time of this writing, is the only commercial airframe manufacturer which has not failed financially. Douglas failed financially and sold out to the McDonnell Company. Lockheed failed and has to secure a government loan. If Boeing fails at some time in the future, then it can be argued that it held out longer.

The Boeing case illustrates coordination problems in a functional design. Let us now look at some problems arising in a project based design.

ORGANIZATION OF A COMPUTER DEPARTMENT

A design change made in the computer operation of a large company illustrates a change toward a matrix form from a project based design. The original computer organization is shown in Figure 26. The organization consisted of about 600 people, 400 of whom were in the data processing center which performed the computation and minor programming for the rest of the organization. Reporting to the director were a technical unit and an administrative unit. The technical unit consisted of computer scientists who evaluated new equipment and new languages, consulted internally on difficult programming and problems, and aided in long-range planning for the department. The administrative unit kept the budgets, costs, and personnel information for the department. The remainder of the organization consisted of, first, about 150 programmers and systems analysts working on three large projects and, second, a unit devoted to small projects and maintenance of on-going systems.

In late 1969, the computer department began to be concerned about the technical quality of its performance. The projects were delivered on time but the work was not well done. In addition, morale and turnover problems appeared among the programmers. After investigating, a task force identified several problems.

Several of these were designated as phase-out problems. Every project, whether it lasts three months or three years, must come to an

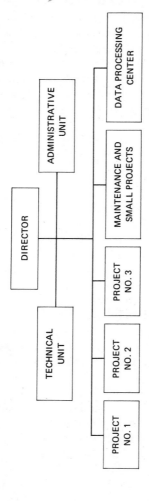

Fig. 26 Original organization of data processing department.

end. This ending or phasing out causes feelings of anxiety on the part of the project members. They are concerned whether they will have a job at the end of the project, and whether their next job will be as interesting, challenging, and responsible as the present one. Therefore many programmers spend a good deal of time looking for their next job. The result was decreased productivity and lower performance on final tasks such as documentation.

A second problem, aggravated by the phase-out, was turnover. An analysis of exit interviews showed that turnover was greatest near the end of a project and occurred because the individual was concerned about his next assignment. Besides incurring the usual turnover costs, the department was concerned because those who left were those who were competent enough to get another job.

The phase-out also caused some skill degradation. Sometimes new projects were not immediately available. The programmers were given what they perceived to be "staff work" or "make work" assignments below their skill level until they could move on to their next project. Worse yet was the tendency for project managers to hold on to skilled personnel. As the manpower requirements declined at the end of the project, the project managers were forced to give up programmers. When they did, the project manager would give up the men he could spare and hold on to the good ones. He did this because the accounting system charged the same for all programmers and if a problem was encountered he couldn't get the good men back. The work required at the end of the project is not as skilled as in the beginning. Therefore people worked below their skill levels. Also they became concerned about the next job. Since they were the last to leave a project, all the better assignments might be gone when they were ready. This problem caused some turnover as well.

Another problem was that insufficient attention was paid to maintaining the skill inventory. The project managers, rightly so, were concerned only with their project. No one was concerned with fitness of programmers to perform projects in the future. Project managers were not concerned with the personal development of the people that worked for them for a short time. This aspect of the job contributed to the anxiety of many programmers. It was not that project managers did not care about people, but that they were primarily concerned with short-run results. This short-run orientation also caused some skill decline. It would pay the project manager to use programmers on tasks for which they already had well-developed skills. A programmer would get to be

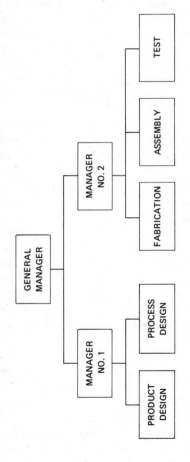

Fig. 27 Data processing after change.

known for being good at a specific task. Every time that task arose he would be asked to do it. While this is good for short-run productivity, it causes skill decay in the unused areas. A technical change might even eliminate the task and make the programmer obsolete.

Most of these problems could be handled by the department manager. However, multiple projects, many programmers, and changing technology require decisions which overload the manager when added to his other duties. In order to handle decisions on how to maintain a supply of skilled resources, the manager introduced two resource integrators as shown in Figure 27. The integrating departments became a home base for systems analysts and programmers respectively. The integrators were primarily concerned with skill mix, maintaining skill levels, and allocation across projects. The allocations were joint decisions between the integrator and project manager. Since the integrators were selected to be competent in their respective areas, they were respected in the allocation process and in the work evaluation process.

There was also a change in the charge for programmers. Three skill categories were established, and charges to projects reflected the skill level. Therefore, project managers had to make skill-cost trade-off decisions. This plan also reduced potential conflict between project managers and integrators. There were still conflicts to be resolved. The project manager had to argue for the priority of his project and his need for a particular skill. The integrator defended the skill level of the individual. Also the integrators tried to eliminate the project manager's fear that if he released a man, he could not get him back. Today this system is not entirely debugged, but it has satisfied its creators.

SUMMARY

This chapter has presented two examples to help illustrate the theory. One example involved a change from a functional structure to a more program-oriented organization. The other was a shift from a project structure to a more functionally oriented design.

NOTE

1. A more complete description and analysis appears in the original article: Jay R. Galbraith, "Environmental and Technological Determinants of Organization Design," in Jay Lorsch and Paul Lawrence (eds.), *Studies in Organization Design* (Homewood, Ill.: Richard D. Irwin, 1970), pp. 113–139.

Chapter 10

AUTHORITY AND RESPONSIBILITY IN LATERAL RELATIONS

The use of lateral relations may solve problems of information overload, but they can create others. When processes cut across lines of authority in organizations, there is always the possibility of obscuring who is responsible for what. A discussion of authority and responsibility is now in order.

AUTHORITY AND RESPONSIBILITY AMBIGUITIES

The use of integrating roles and other lateral relations violates the unity-of-command principle of the classical management theorists and creates role conflict and stress for the individual. This is particularly true for the matrix design, which builds in a dual reporting relation. The prediction of the management theorists was that the lack of a clear-cut, single line of authority would result in organizational ineffectiveness. Since most early knowledge about organizations came from the military operating under battle conditions, it is easy to see how one would predict that multiple authority would lead to ineffectiveness. But what about the effects of multiple authority in organizations with high uncertainty and unstructured situations?

There is no evidence to indicate that multiple authority and role conflict lead to ineffectiveness. This fact is partly due to the lack of work on the subject, but the studies that are available do not support the assertion. The work of Marquis and of Goodman suggest that the response of organizations to multiple authority relations is one of ambiguous definition of who is responsible.[1] It is even suggested by some project managers that ambiguity is the best response.

> One project manager observed, for example, that one of his subordinates may have most of his authority and interest in design. He will also have other interests and perhaps some authority in other areas such as launch, quality control, or production. It is meaningless, he said, to try to define precisely areas of authority in order to prevent gaps or overlaps. For example, when his chief of design finds a realtively free moment and there are important problems in quality control, he is expected to help those directly responsible to solve them. This project manager further observed: "If you rigidly define authority, all you do is leave holes in the organization through which the big problems fall. However, if you go along with a 'Gaussian' distribution of authority, the overlaps insure that all problems are considered by someone."[2]

There is considerable evidence of the existence of role conflict in professional organizations, both from multiple authority relations and from the conflicting influences of administrative goals and professional standards.[3] Thus for organizations performing uncertain tasks, there is widespread existence of multiple authority relations and role conflict, but there is no evidence that ambiguity results in ineffectiveness, and some people even assert that ambiguity is good.

Like many other concepts about which there is no evidence and many strong, experience-based feelings, the effects of multiple authority depend on the conditions under which it is applied. If this is true, what are the various conditions? The first condition is the one already mentioned—the nature of the task. In many organizational operations, time is of the essence. There is no time for exploration and negotiation. It is not advantageous to see who has the most information relevant to a decision. The important thing is to act and act fast. Under these conditions, a single, clear line of authority is needed. Many military, production, and operating situations fall into this category. If there is only minimal time pressure, then search processes can be undertaken to obtain relevant information. Here the issue is to see that the best decision gets made, and there is less concern for who makes it or how fast. Under these conditions, multiple authority can be effective if the conflicts are resolved in a problem solving manner.

The second condition involves making use of the fact that individuals vary in their ability to handle role conflicts, and roles vary in the amount of conflict to which they are subject. Role conflict has been shown to produce anxiety and stress in the individual who has reduced satisfaction with the role.[4] Individuals vary considerably in how they cope with the conflict. The marginal man studies suggest that some individuals perform the linking, conflict-laden roles quite well and are satisfied with them.[5] Likewise, some individuals handle the dual reporting relation with minimal difficulty. Almost all of us were raised in the dual authority system of the family, so dual authority is not completely foreign. However, there are individuals for whom such a position would be unbearable. The organization needs to match linking roles with individuals who have a high tolerance for stress and ambiguity.

The third necessary condition for effective use of multiple authority is a problem solving climate. Role conflict, like other conflicts mentioned previously, can be good or bad depending on how they are resolved. The project manager quoted previously can use ambiguity and multiple authority if his project team is more concerned with the problem than with the structure and who solves it. Solving the problem has to be more important than winning, controlling, or selling your solution. His quotation indicates that he thinks effectiveness can be improved more by emphasizing teamwork and problem solving than by role definition.

The best way to create a climate for reducing the negative aspects of role conflict is to maintain open communication for the sharing and confronting of conflicts. Walton points out:

> We increasingly understand that psychological and social energy is tied up in suppressing conflict, that conflicts not confronted may be played out in indirect and destructive ways, and that the differences that underlie interpersonal conflict often represent diversity or complementarity of significant potential value to the organization. An interpersonal or organizational system that can acknowledge and effectively confront its internal conflicts has a greater capacity to innovate and adapt.[6]

Such a system can also reduce the negative aspects of role conflict for the affected individual.

The implication of this section so far is that a manager whose departments engage in lateral relations can improve effectiveness more by creating a problem solving climate than by clarifying role definition. In one sense this is true, but in another it is not. It is true that little can be gained by increasing role definition *as we have traditionally defined roles.* Traditionally, most organizations have responded to information overloads by setting up self-contained units. This strategy allowed them to utilize competitive, free-market cultural values inside the organization. However, individual responsibility and competition were effective motivating forces only if there was little need for cooperation between roles. To the degree that interdependence could be self-contained, then all the ambiguity, uncertainty, and conflict were contained within a single role. If self-containment was not feasible, individual responsibility could still be maintained, but only if areas of jurisdiction could be precisely defined. This was feasible for predictable, repetitive tasks or ones for which a dominant operational goal could be found. Therefore personnel departments undertook the preparation of elaborate job descriptions and organization charts. If there was still an overlap or gap, the issue was raised to the next level in the hierarchy where a single role could be found. All these devices precisely defined the areas of jurisdiction, and since interdependence, conflict, and ambiguity were confined to a single role, there was no concern for the process of resolving these issues. They were resolved with the best integrating mechanism of all— the human brain. Since some people were better than others at resolving conflict, the process was controlled by selecting those who were better. Thus role definition and selection were the most important personnel management processes.

Today, and in the future, the picture is different for many tasks. Potential sources of conflict cannot be structured or defined away into a single role. Specialization results in interdependence between roles. High technology causes enough uncertainty that areas of jurisdiction cannot be defined ahead of time. In some organizations, such as the multinational one, there is always something wrong with any structure it chooses—product, geographic, or function. All these facts force organizations to work laterally. Since ambiguity and conflict exist between rather than within roles, more attention has to be given to the *process of resolving conflicts between roles.* Instead of removing the sources of conflict with role definition, the task of the personnel function is to help their organizations confront conflicts. This is done not by defining areas of jurisdiction but by defining roles with respect to the process of decision making and conflict resolution. This is illustrated by our previous quotation from a project manager. He said it is impossible to define roles in the sense of areas of jurisdiction, but he is quite clear about the kinds of role behavior he expects. He is not ambiguous about role definition concerning the behaviors in the decision process. Thus there is a need for role definition, but lateral relations require different role definitions from those which support individual responsibility.

The organization cannot get rid of ambiguity. It is inherent in every task. Traditionally, and in many current organizations performing predictable tasks, ambiguity was concentrated within the role. The role occupant was faced with stresses caused by role overloads and priorities of diverse task elements. Today's tasks involving high technology and specialization still have the same conflicts of priority, but now the conflicts are between roles. Organizations have always left priority questions unresolved until the best information was available to resolve them. But now the resolution requires interpersonal rather than intrapersonal processes. Some of the emphasis on team building derives from the fact that organizations must explicitly deal with the role definition process across roles.

The technology of team building is still being developed. It is still developing a new definition of individual responsibility. The individual does not "go it alone," but neither is the individual to be lost in "group think" processes. In athletics, our society has a demonstration of the way individuals are rewarded for team contribution. In organizations, there is not the clear goal and outside threat to motivate teamwork.

RESPONSIBILITY CHARTING

A useful technique for use in team building activities and role definition is the responsibility chart.[7] This has been used for a long time in defining jurisdictional areas. However it is more useful in resolving ambiguities in decision processes and identifying areas in which ambiguities must remain until more information is available.

This process begins by identifying the specific decisions that have to be made at a particular level of the organization. The list of decisions, which should not be so detailed as to overwhelm the group, should be listed in rows, as shown in Figure 28. Along the top of the table are listed

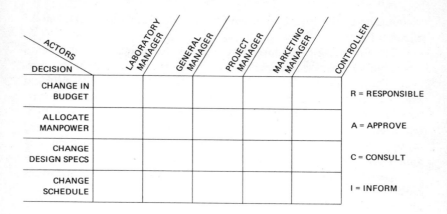

Fig. 28   Example of responsibility chart.

the participants in the decision processes listed along the side. Now it is a matter of simply matching the participants to the decision process. The degree of participation can be indicated by any set of words that is meaningful for the organization. For example, one role could be specifically responsible for a particular decision. Another role would not be responsible but must approve any decision made. Another need not approve but should be consulted. Still another need not be consulted but should be informed if any change is made. These degrees of participation can be indicated by R,A,C, and I respectively.

To use the chart, the participants first identify major decision areas. Then each one fills out the form privately. The results are aggregated and presented to the group. The responses are not associated with any individual. Almost every time this is done, there will be wide variance in the responses as to who is responsible for what. This fact in itself is quite revealing. The remainder of the meeting is concerned with the gaps and overlaps. Dual responsibilities can be built in if needed. The result of the process is a completed chart that is jointly agreed upon by all participants. It is more meaningful than organization charts and job descriptions. The conflicts are confronted before all concerned and resolved to the extent possible. A follow-up meeting is then scheduled for three to six months in the future to reconsider the decision process and make changes in it.

The foregoing procedure is very useful for new teams or when a change of structure is introduced. The conflicts are going to arise sometime. They might as well be confronted early before a specific problem arises. In this way there is an avoidance of blame and finger-pointing. The process eliminates as many role ambiguities as possible and highlights areas that will remain ambiguous. Since not all decisions need groups, the group can decide upon procedures or criteria for determining which decisions require group inputs.

Many consulting firms have used this approach. Some organizations have had bad experiences with it, but their problem lies with the organization climate, not the technique. One should separate improper use of a technique from the technique itself.

SUMMARY

This last chapter has presented some discussion of the authority-responsibility problems that arise when lateral relations are used. The problems have always been present in organizations but are accentuated with the presence of integrating roles. The factors discussed in this chapter can very easily become the limiting factors unless they are confronted in some type of organization development program.

CONCLUDING REMARKS

This concludes the formal presentation of the organization design framework. However, a few additional concluding remarks seem to be appropriate. A major portion of the book has been devoted to organic or so-called matrix forms of organization. These forms are not new. Teams, or committees if you prefer, project managers, and dual authority relations have been used for some time. This book has tried to tie together some of those concepts like matrix structure, on line–real time systems, autonomous groups, etc., so that they can be seen as part of a larger scheme. In this manner they appear as alternative designs or complementary changes to facilitate the same design. The framework or larger scheme is what the author has tried to communicate in this book. He believes that it is only through this kind of framework that people who have the same problem can communicate. If not this framework, then some other framework is needed to permit communication between the computer systems analyst, the behavioral scientist, and the manager.

Since the book rises or falls with the framework the reader should be aware of its limitations. First, it has not been specifically tested. The framework is consistent with most of the available empirical evidence and the author is unaware of any evidence which refutes the implicit hypotheses. But there has not been a program of research which tests the framework.

Second, the framework has little room for new structures. When viewed objectively the so-called matrix designs are really patchwork on what is still the basic bureaucratic structure with hierarchically distributed power. Part of the problem comes from using comparative studies as a basis for theory construction. That means that the theorist is limited to the experiments that managers are willing to create. Since most managers do not create radically new forms, the theorist is limited in the range of variation he can observe. The framework is similarly limited. If interested in genuinely new designs, the author himself must step outside of the framework.

These remarks are intended to create a healthy respect for the limitations of the framework, not to destroy the reader's confidence in it. The reader has my assurance that I would make choices exactly as I describe them.

NOTES

1. D. G. Marquis and D. M. Straight, "Organizational Factors in Project Performance," Sloan School of Management Working Paper No. 133–65; and Richard Goodman, "Ambiguous Authority Definition in Project Management," *Academy of Management Journal,* December 1967, pp. 395–408.
2. George Steiner and William Ryan, *Industrial Project Management* (New York: Macmillan, 1968), p. 32.
3. Alan Filley and Robert House, *Managerial Process and Organization Behavior* (Glenview, Ill.: Scott Foresman, 1969), Chapter 13.
4. Robert Kahn, Donald Wolfe, Robert Quinn, J. Diedrick Snoek, and Robert Rosenthal, *Organizational Stress: Studies in Role Conflict and Ambiguity* (New York: John Wiley, 1964).
5. R. C. Ziller, B. J. Stark, and H. O. Pruden, "Marginality and Integrative Management Positions," *Academy of Management Journal,* December 1969, pp. 487–495.

6. Richard Walton, *Interpersonal Peacemaking: Confrontations and Third Party Consultation* (Reading, Mass.: Addison-Wesley, 1969).
7. Robert Melcher, "Roles and Relationships: Clarifying the Manager's Job," *Personnel,* May-June 1967, reprinted in David Cleland and William King, *Systems, Organizations, Analysis Management: A Book of Readings* (New York: McGraw-Hill, 1969), pp. 365–371.